MPUS MINISTRY

The Single Life
A Christian Challenge

Martha M. Niemann

LIGUORI
PUBLICATIONS

One Liguori Drive
Liguori, Missouri 63057
(314) 464-2500

Imprimi Potest:
John F. Dowd, C.SS.R.
Provincial, St. Louis Province
Redemptorist Fathers

Imprimatur:
+ Edward J. O'Donnell
Vicar General, Archdiocese of St. Louis

ISBN 0-89243-254-3
Library of Congress Catalog Card Number: 86-81335
Cover design by Joann M. Koharchik
Copyright © 1986, Martha M. Niemann
Printed in U.S.A.

Scripture texts used in this work are taken from the NEW AMERICAN BIBLE, copyright © 1970, by the Confraternity of Christian Doctrine, Washington, D.C., and are used by permission of copyright owner. All rights reserved.

Dedicated to

Martha J. Curtis
with love

Table of Contents

The Challenges of Single Life

Growing in My Relationship with Jesus

Looking Ahead

Acknowledgments

With deep appreciation I acknowledge the people who helped the dream of this book become reality.

I begin by thanking my parents, grandparents, sisters, brothers, and their spouses and children for nurturing the seed of faith that God planted in me. I thank the religious Sisters and priests who taught me, counseled me, and urged me to keep searching and listening, especially my spiritual director Sister Marian Hahn, R.C., who has intimately shared my spiritual journey for the past three and a half years.

I thank the friends who have stood by me with prayer and moral support as I endured the labor pains of giving birth to this book, especially my sister and confidante, Emily Burak, and my prayer partner, Peggy Schaeffer, and my listener extraordinaire, Margaret Klopfenstein. The input I received from other single Christians was invaluable. I thank those I know only through their letters and those I know as friends. I especially acknowledge my "dinner group," who patiently listened to me read parts of the book to them and brainstormed chapter 11 with me on a hot summer night.

The rough draft of this manuscript was reviewed by three individuals who lovingly and gently gave me their editorial comments and encouraged me to stretch a little bit more — Rita Dwyer, Marianne Hanton, and Father Bob Keffer. The writing and editing was made easier because of the word processor at my disposal, thanks to the generosity of my employer.

I thank the people of Liguori Publications for their professional advice and loving affirmation. I affectionately acknowledge Father Norman Muckerman, C.SS.R., who first said to me, "You may have the makings of a book." I fondly remember this book's first editor, Roger Marchand. I trust he and the Lord are turning the pages together in heaven.

Finally, I thank the many people who have revealed the living, loving Jesus to me over the years and inspired me to grow in my relationship with him. To them I say, "If you see yourself in a chapter, I am giving you my verbal hug of appreciation."

MMN
April 29, 1986

Foreword

The word *single* conjures up many images. There are singles who have never been married and those who are single again because of divorce or death. There are singles with dependent children and singles with dependent parents. There are young singles, old singles, and singles in-between.

Thinking about the diverse types of people who read this book, I initially became overwhelmed. *How,* I wondered, *can I begin to relate my single experiences to everyone?* The answer that came to me was, *I can't, but Jesus can.*

There you have it — I am trusting Jesus to speak to your heart.

I do not presume that my feelings are the same as yours. Some chapters will touch upon your experience, others will not. You may feel I left out something, but it might not have been part of my life. This book contains personal and prayerful reflections on my own life as a Christian single and as a single Christian.

So let me clarify where I am coming from. You may be twenty or fifty. I am thirty. You may live with your parents or in an apartment with a roommate. I own my townhouse and live alone, 600 miles from my family. You may work in a school, a factory, a hospital. I work in an office. You may have chosen the single life as a vocation. I am still not sure.

Many externals of our lives may differ. Because we are Christian, however, we share a faith and common search that binds us together — a search for a deeper relationship with Jesus Christ. We share this search with our married and religious sisters and brothers. But the fact that we are single adds dimensions to the search that are unique to us.

To be single and searching for Jesus is the theme of this book, as it has been the theme of my life. I have divided this theme into three parts: The Challenges of Single Life, Growing in My Relationship with Jesus, and Looking Ahead. If you read this book from beginning to end, my search will unfold for you as it has unfolded in my life. Each chapter stands on its own, so you may choose to read whatever chapter piques your interest whenever you happen to pick up the book.

The chapters are short for a reason. I share events in my life that have stimulated my search. I ask questions, pose answers, then close. My purpose is to let you know you are not alone in your feelings or to help you stretch and think about something in a new way. I then leave you to think, to pray, to search for your own answers, and to integrate them as Jesus is calling you to integrate them into your life and your relationship with him.

We may lead very different lives, but because we believe in the same Lord and Savior we have the most important common denominator there is — Jesus Christ. Let's search together for a deeper understanding of his presence in our lives. Let's pray for his Spirit of sharing heart to heart. Through this shared search, may we grow closer to Jesus, to each other, and to *all* our sisters and brothers.

PART ONE

THE
CHALLENGES
OF SINGLE LIFE

1

To Be
a Single Christian

Living a Christian single life in our worldly, couple-oriented society is a challenge. Because it is such a challenge, I need to share my life with other singles who understand and relate to my ups and downs. I also need to read about how others rise to the challenge of living their single lives as followers of Jesus.

Since the single population is burgeoning these days, there is plenty written in the secular press about and for singles. But maybe you feel, as I do, that an essential ingredient is often missing: depth — and specifically, the spiritual depth brought about through a loving, growing relationship with Jesus Christ.

Popular periodicals and books skim the surface of single life. They give hints, for example, on how to cook for one. What about how to cope with eating alone? I know what it feels like to sit home on a Saturday night without a date. What about attending Sunday morning Mass without a family?

On the positive side, singles have lots of free time to do their "own thing," and the secular press tends to emphasize dating, travel, and hobbies. But what about those of us who choose altruistic activities to fill our free time, like serving in a soup kitchen, volunteering at a problem-pregnancy center, or baby-sitting, weekends at a time, for a friend's children?

The secular press seems to draw disproportionate attention to the extremes of single life. To be single is to be stereotyped either as a "lonely heart" or a "swinging single." These stereotypes are limiting and unjust. They also tend to discourage me from sharing my life and opening my heart with those who are not single.

Why? I am afraid people will assume I am a "lonely heart" if I mention the word *loneliness*. If I talk about my latest travels and favorite restaurants, I am equally afraid I will be perceived to be a superficial swinger. The truth of the matter is that I am neither, yet I am both. There must be other singles who are living this paradox!

To be single is to be a lonely heart and a swinger. It is to live the life of the mundane and glamorous, of sadness and joy, of isolation and community, of disappointment and fulfillment. It is to be detached and intimate, emotional and rational, businesslike and personal, social, sexual, and spiritual too. Being single is being all these things *and more*. For us who are believers in Jesus Christ, to be single is to respond to Jesus' call to look for a deeper, Christ-centered purpose and meaning in our singleness.

It is natural, then, to turn to the religious press for the Christian perspective lacking in the secular press. Turn to the religious press I did, only to be disappointed. I searched Christian bookstore after parish magazine rack for articles and books addressing the life-style and spirituality unique to the single life. I found very little that was current or relevant to me or today's society. I felt frustrated and cheated. Where else could I look?

My search did not end in futility. Rather, my frustration sparked a new search — a soul search. Could it be that God was calling me to fill a void and write for my peers who, like me, are also hungering for support and sustenance in living a Christian single life?

Initially, the risk involved in responding to this call over-whelmed me. In time, I gave in to the gentle promptings from within and began to write. The *Liguorian* magazine published several of my articles and took a survey of its readership. The response confirmed what I felt. Other single Christians were searching as I was.

I take the risk of opening my heart, both in sorrow and in joy, to write about the very things I have longed to read about. On paper, I become vulnerable by sharing what my relationship with Jesus is, how I draw nearer to him and sometimes drift, even run, away from him.

I begin by swallowing my pride and admitting, as I rarely do, I am a lonely heart. There are down times when I just wish someone would hug me or send me a letter or be receptive to my spontaneous "I love you."

But don't jump to any one-sided conclusions. I am a swinger

too. I enjoy jetting off to a new city to meet new people, to give a speech, to see the sights, free from any obligations on my home front. I love a date for dinner and dancing, with all the glamour and fantasy of a good romance novel.

Yet, I am quick to interject feelings and experiences that do not fall into either the lonely heart or swinger categories. I cherish my home, and am deeply touched and honored when my family — parents and married siblings included — choose to travel to my home for Thanksgiving. While I enjoy my home full of people, I also am possessive of my time at home alone. I know and appreciate how silence beckons me to pray, to be still and to relate intimately with my Lord Jesus.

During such quiet times with Jesus I have been given a deeper insight into the person God created me to be and is calling me to become. God is calling me, and every believer, to be as Jesus prays in John's Gospel:

> . . . that all may be one
> as you, Father, are in me, and I in you;
> I pray that they may be [one] in us . . .
> that their unity may be complete.
> So shall the world know that you sent me....
> (John 17:21,23)

Jesus is calling us to "be one" — to be one with him, his Father, and the Holy Spirit, to be one with our true selves, and to be one with the people and the world around us.

To be one is Jesus' gift and call to every Christian. It is a gift and mystery to be united in peace and purpose with our God. It is a call and a lifelong challenge to be in touch and at peace with the self deep within us, where we are united intimately with God. It is our mission to bring this gift of peace and unity to everyone and everything in our lives.

While this gift and call to oneness is extended to everyone, regardless of state of life or health, to be single and to be one with Jesus sums up what it means to me to be a single Christian.

Let's reflect on our lives in the light of Jesus' call to oneness. Together may we become one, may our unity be complete, so that the world will know Jesus sent us.

2

The Single Mystique

The single status is surrounded by an aura of mystery. Despite the increase in numbers of singles and singles-again in the American population, there still exists what I call a "single mystique."

The single mystique is typified by an attitude which seems to assume that being single is merely a temporary passage from childhood to a more "acceptable" state of adulthood. It implies that not being married is a failure of sorts and that choosing to be single is an idiosyncrasy. It presumes that to be single is to be incomplete and unfulfilled.

This mystique seems to be perpetuated by everyone — strangers, our loved ones, and ourselves. People who ask "Why isn't a nice girl like you married?" probably think they are being complimentary. What response can singles give to this question, especially if in their heart of hearts they want to be married and also wonder why they are not? This question could be received as "What's wrong with you?" Many singles have a poor self-image because they have internalized an attitude that being unmarried is somehow "wrong."

Words like *unmarried, premarital,* and *unattached* in themselves contribute to the mystique. It's like describing life as "pre-death" or joy as "un-sadness."

My personal relationships with family and friends are affected by the single mystique. People are quick to ask me about my job, but no one ever seems to ask me about my life — my friends, my leisure time, my daily routine. When I offer such information, desiring to share my life and not just my work, I often receive nonverbal hints that say, "I don't want to hear about this," or "I can't relate, so don't tell me."

I most often sense people wanting to change the subject when I share my loneliness with people who are married. Maybe they feel uncomfortable because they can't offer a solution. I know there are no quick fixes to loneliness. I just wish they would be present to me and listen.

Sharing my desire to marry with a married friend or family member, I often hear: "Married life isn't all bliss." I always want to counter with, "I never said it was; single life isn't all bliss either."

There was a time when I was hurt by such reactions, but no more. I have come to accept that it is hard for people to imagine what being single or living alone is like, and they may be afraid to ask. I have also learned to be more sensitive to their situations. They may be unhappy or frustrated in their married or religious lives, and may assume the grass is greener as a single.

I still struggle with feeling like the odd one out. As I grow older, I am finding more and more of my friends are married. To be with them is to be with their spouses and their children. I enjoy these additions to my life, but the reality of my singleness cannot be denied, and my circle of single friends seems to be diminishing. This phenomenon also is occurring in my family. There are now more married siblings than single ones. It was one thing to be the "senior single" in the family because all the younger ones were still too young to be married, but now the younger ones are growing older and marrying.

If all these words, feelings, and situations in our society add up to a "single mystique," how can we Christian singles deal with it?

First, I think we must quit fighting it and accept it. It is part of nature to mate. It is part of human nature to desire a partner and to become emotionally and physically attached to that partner. It follows, then, that our society is based on couples and families.

If we accept what is human, then we must turn to what is divine for the affirmation that we need as singles. That means turning to Jesus for the understanding, the compassion, and the listening presence that we need when we feel left out of our couple-oriented society.

The Jesus who walked this earth acknowledged the integrity of the single life by the very life he lived — the single life. The Jesus who walks with us today continues to acknowledge the single life.

He helps us experience an inner integrity and sense of fulfillment as we grow into the whole persons his Father created us to be.

Through my deepening relationship with Jesus, I am able to fight the temptation to internalize the "single mystique." I am at peace about being single. Jesus assures me there is nothing wrong with me because I am not married. Although it is good and natural to want to be married, I am not weird if I remain single the rest of my life.

Jesus teaches us to live each present moment to the fullest. To be caught up in the "single mystique" is to live in the future, to live for the day when we might marry. That day may never come. In the meantime, we must live in the here-and-now world, accepting and treasuring each moment of our single lives as a gift from God. If and when God calls us to the married life, that, too, will be his gift to us.

Lastly, Jesus encourages us to share our single lives with other Christian single and married people. Other Christian singles can provide that positive human understanding and peer support that we justifiably crave. They can empathize with the challenges of being single and being Christian in today's society. And married Christians will come to understand us and embrace us if we open up and share our hearts with them.

Perhaps, in time, and with the help of God's grace, we will dispel the "single mystique" and come to acknowledge, as Jesus did, the integrity of single life.

3

Do Singles
Fit in the Church?

It is one thing to learn to accept being "left out" of our secular, couple-oriented society. It is quite another thing to feel "left out" in the Church we call the family of God. Yet, I have felt forgotten by the Church, and so have many other singles who have shared with me in person and in letters.

More than once I have heard, "I want to be needed and wanted in the Church community." Or, "I have money and time and no place to channel them." A remark that took me by surprise was this one: "My parish census form didn't even have a 'single' category to check off!"

As singles, we crave to be noticed by our couple-oriented Christian community. Many of us find ourselves in parishes that are so family-oriented in their liturgies, homilies, activities, and budgets that we feel ignored and overlooked.

We want to feel included in the Church. Many of us are living alone, far from family, sometimes in large, impersonal cities and work environments. We may be detached and on our own, but we still yearn for some sense of "roots," and we feel that the Church is an ideal place to look for it.

We also know that being Christian entails being aware of, and active in, a world beyond our immediate concerns. We may be involved in our personal careers or extended-family obligations, yet we know we need to mix and mingle with the broad spectrum of human life and lifestyles. Too often our own private lives cut us off from the beauty and pain of human existence: the beauty found in the giggle of a baby, the pride of a parent, the memories of a senior citizen; the pain seen in the struggles of the handicapped, the hunger of the poor, and the loneliness of the shut-in. Isn't it natural to hope our Christian brothers and sisters will help us broaden our vision and stir us to service? But they don't even seem to acknowledge our presence among them.

Even as we yearn to be identified as singles within our Christian communities, we also want to be embraced as people who are really no different from our married and religious brothers and sisters. Do we not all share the common desire and effort to grow closer to God and to spread his Good News in word and deed throughout our world? We are not oddities because we are single. We are Christians who happen to be single.

Where do we singles fit in the Church? This question stirs additional and even more thought-provoking ones: Do we expect too much of the Church? Are we giving enough of ourselves to make *the* Church *our* Church?

I really don't doubt that we fit. In Baptism, God made us members of his family on earth, and representatives of this family welcomed us into the Church. I belong to this family as much as anyone who sits in the pew next to me, behind me, or across the aisle. God calls each of us individually to his altar. I, like my married and religious peers, have responded.

Since Jesus calls us as individuals, I believe he calls us to treat each other accordingly. Maybe the Church is as guilty as secular society in categorizing people and then ''writing them off'' when they don't conform to a norm — in this case, the married/family norm.

Are we not, as individuals and as Church, called to follow Jesus' example of seeing God's Spirit in every person regardless of external appearances? Jesus touched lepers, dined with tax collectors, and befriended prostitutes. He taught us by example what it means to accept and love people as they are and to affirm them into becoming all that God created them to be.

As singles, we can do our part by letting go of the question, ''Where do I fit?'' Jesus has already made us members of his family. It is up to each of us to act like one of the family, even when the family fails to acknowledge us. It is up to us to get involved. That means joining in parish activities, those for singles and those for the broader Church community as well.

In my parish, many singles are involved in the Young Adults Club and the ''Over 30'' singles group, but they are also acting as extraordinary ministers, lectors, Confirmation teachers, and catechumenate sponsors. They act as chaperons at the city's shelters for the homeless, and they serve on the Social Concerns Committee which, among other things, distributes food to the needy.

Personally, I feel I fit in the Church when I make the effort to become involved. Belonging to several parishes over the years, I have noticed my feelings of discomfort and detachment emerge whenever I am not active in a parish group or ministry. When I first joined my current parish I participated in the Young Adults Club activities. Then I changed jobs, and my business travel schedule impinged on my parish participation. My feeling of being detached from the Church grew.

Coming to grips with this feeling, I decided to join one of the parish folk groups which made allowances for my periodic absences. Within two months of singing with the group, my sense of community was restored. I felt welcomed by this group. Later, by participating in the parishwide choir for Holy Week, I met more people and new friendships developed.

I have learned through experience that a sense of belonging and involvement go hand in hand. I have also learned that as I mingle with my fellow parishioners and share myself with them I raise their consciousness about single Christians without "singling" myself out.

While the hierarchical Church doesn't seem to address the single vocation or lifestyle with much enthusiasm or interest, I am encouraged by recent references to singles in homilies and in the Prayer of the Faithful at Mass. I am heartened by the pastoral and lay support being given young adult and singles groups in many parishes and some dioceses.

Singles do fit in the Church. Our desire to feel included is legitimate. We have the right to expect Christ's Body — the Church — to embrace us as Christ embraces us all. At the same time we must participate, we must open up, we must persevere. As one single wrote to me, "Instead of leaving the Church that has forgotten me, I will stay, be active, and hope they find and love me someday."

Let's hang in there. Let's strive to love as Jesus loves us, so that we, the Church, will someday embrace everyone and ultimately become the family Jesus envisioned us to be.

4

Far from
Loved Ones

A knot rose in my throat as I watched the family station wagon drive out of sight, leaving me standing alone on a crowded city street. I was excited about beginning my career and living in my own apartment, but I was saddened by the thought of living 250 miles from my family.

The reality of my new living situation sank in slowly. I periodically caught myself coming home from work and looking for a message on the memo board. How's that for a habit that dies hard? It obviously took my heart longer to adjust to what my head could not deny. I was living alone, and that meant no more messages on the memo board.

The habit of checking for messages was part of life in my family of seven children. The memo board was a permanent fixture on the refrigerator door. As a teenager, I had been more interested in the messages on the outside of the refrigerator than the possible treats on the inside — that is, if there was a message from a friend and not a reminder of a chore to be done. If no one was home — a rare occasion — a message on the memo board said someone still cared. Living alone, I found neither loved ones at home nor the daily notes to remind me that someone cared.

Two hundred and fifty miles really isn't that far away, and I quickly learned I could catch a train home Friday night after work, enjoy a weekend with the family, and even squeeze in a football game with college friends. Sleeping the five hours on the return trip to the city helped me report to work on Monday morning at least somewhat rested.

It wasn't long before I noticed a new habit forming. It is what a friend calls the ''PDBs'' — the Pre-Departure Blues. This syndrome strikes when I get ready to leave home. It hits anywhere between one to four hours before the scheduled time of departure, before the scheduled time of being whisked away from loved ones once again. The symptoms can be anything from complete silence to sarcasm or a grouchy demeanor.

My PDBs often manifested themselves in extreme sensitivity. It was as if I didn't want anyone to touch me or talk to me. One of my brothers, who also lived far from loved ones, was labeled "The Big Brown Bear" by the family. He seemed to growl just before departure.

Good-byes were difficult. I wonder if I did not subconsciously try to make them easier by stirring up trouble so that everyone, including myself, was glad to see me go. In the end, I only made matters worse. Time and again, on the train I found myself feeling guilty and even lonelier because of the discord I had created as I left.

Now that I am aware of the PDBs, I warn my family and ask for their understanding and assistance at departure. I am working on a new habit of taking some quiet time to pack and pray in those final pre-departure hours. Packing is a prerequisite for leaving and so is praying, if I hope to make my leaving loving.

When I moved more than 500 miles from my family, my sense of separation from them intensified. The additional miles between us meant less frequent trips home. This move also coincided with the arrival of nieces and nephews on the family scene. With little ones to watch grow, my yearning to see family deepened, even as the distance between us lengthened.

Flying home to stand up as my nephew's godmother at his baptism, I became aware of another form of PDBs — *Post*-Departure Blues. With no vacation time to take, I had departed from the office on Friday afternoon and took an early-bird special flight back on Monday morning. In the blink of an eye, I was back at my desk, feeling blue because I was once again 500 miles from loved ones.

After months of separation it truly had been a joy to see everyone again, but I felt lonelier than I had been before I left. Struggling with my emotions, I did what I often do: I searched for an analogy that might explain them to me. I found one.

The analogy is simple. My weekend at home was like inviting a starving woman to sit at a banquet table but only allowing her to taste a tiny sample from each dish. I was given morsels of each delicacy — hugs and kisses included — but was forced to leave the table before I had my fill. After leaving the "table," I felt my hunger more acutely. I seemed to miss my family more after a taste of togetherness than I had during my deprivation of the previous months.

Whether the separation from loved ones is typified by no messages on the memo board, pre-departure blues, or the unsatisfied hunger accentuated by short, infrequent visits, the reality is that it is hard to live far from loved ones. How do we, as Christian singles, deal with this reality?

Maybe we should begin by asking, "Do I have to live so far away?" Some people have no choice. Others make the choice because of career, personal preference, or a sense that God wants them where they are. If we have a choice and feel extremely lonesome for loved ones, maybe it is time to consider moving closer to them. But if we don't have a choice, or our choice is to remain where we are, then what? Regardless of choice, the longing in our hearts is real.

Communication is one of the best ways to overcome this longing. Letters in the mailbox become those messages on the memo board. Receiving letters implies writing letters. Ma Bell advertises that the telephone is the next best thing to being there. While my budget is tight, I make allowances for those necessary phone calls to keep in touch.

I have reminded my loved ones that the phone rings in both directions. When they countered that I am seldom home, my parents remedied the situation by giving me an answering machine for Christmas. It is a great replacement for the memo board.

But what about the blues that come pre-departure, post-departure, and in-between departures? Day-to-day intimacy and interaction with parents, sisters, brothers, nieces, nephews, and hometown friends can no longer be, but I have felt love transcend the miles that separate us. In many ways I feel distance has strengthened my bond with my loved ones. There is a tendency sometimes to take people for granted when we see them every day. Because of the blues of separation, I hold my family in greater esteem and cherish our time together.

Through the endurance of this separation, my relationship with God has deepened. Regardless of how near or far my family is, I have come to recognize the hunger in my heart that even loved ones cannot fill. I have learned that God, and God alone, fills the void deep within that I feel but cannot articulate.

Recognizing this, I can now miss my loved ones and allow my feelings to hurt. Once I have given myself the permission to feel blue, I am reminded to turn to God and to be honest with him about my feelings. Through this process I have become more aware of my dependence upon God as my loving Father, my friend and confidant Jesus, and the Holy Spirit within me.

My loneliness prods me to turn to God, to give him my heart. Missing my loved ones brings them to mind and, subsequently, to my prayer. By remembering family and friends during Mass, I feel a special communion with them. This sense of communion with faraway loved ones has deepened my appreciation of the communion we have with all believers, living and dead, near and far.

Finally, as I have moved from place to place, farther from my real family, God has given me many loving families and friends with whom to share life's journey. These new loved ones have embraced me as their own, inviting me to holiday meals, remembering my birthday, and doing any number of things that are typically done by and with those we love.

Through all my moves, I have experienced the truth of Jesus' words in Mark 10:29-30: "I give you my word, there is no one who has given up home, brothers or sisters, mother or father, children or property, for me and for the gospel who will not receive in this present age a hundred times as many homes, brothers and sisters, mothers, children and property — and persecution besides — and in the age to come, everlasting life."

Even as I periodically experience the "persecution" of missing family and friends, I have learned I am really never far from loved ones because God is always with me and is constantly expanding my circle of loved ones wherever I go.

5

No One Knows
When I Come
and Go

Living alone has its ups and downs, and so does living with
roommates. I have tried both arrangements. For the past five years
my preference has been to live alone.

The freedom of living alone has meant forfeiting the companionship of roommates. It also has meant dealing with the
isolation I feel because no one knows when I come and go.

That's the head's way of phrasing it. If I am feeling particularly
low, I hear my heart say, "No one *cares* when I come and go." I
know this is a self-centered and ridiculous attitude, but periodically it plays on my mind, especially when things happen that
focus my attention on my isolated situation.

In the fall of 1982 I was unemployed. Because of unemployment compensation, my financial worries were of less concern to
me than my emotions. I had to psych myself up for every job
interview and, then, not let myself sink too far when I was
rejected. Without a roommate or a spouse, I had no one to reassure
me or listen to me.

I also had to deal with the fact that no one, *absolutely no one,*
noticed my presence or absence on a day-to-day basis. When I was
working and failed to show up at the office, someone would call to
check on me, sometimes waking the sleepyhead who had missed
her alarm. Without a job, I was expected nowhere by no one.

It was during this transition period that I first honestly faced the
real isolation that comes with living alone. Fortunately, at this
point in my life my relationship with Jesus was developing, and I
turned to him with my feelings. At the same time I dropped a note

in the mail to my parents saying, "If for some reason you need to reach me and can't, then call the following people . . . " and I gave them a list.

While this message was meant to say what it did, it was also my way of trying to communicate something else. Without coming right out and saying so, I wanted my family to know that I needed someone to keep an eye on me. When I eventually confided in some close friends that I was fearful that something might happen to me and no one would know, they periodically checked in on me. That lasted only until I found a job.

Another incident occurred that reminded me of my isolated situation. An ice storm incapacitated the city one Friday night. I was able to get as far as my friend's house where I was forced to spend the night. Her phone rang off the hook until her locally based family — daughter, son, and sister — checked in on her. I commented to her at the time, "How nice to know people are watching out for you."

When I left my friend the next afternoon, her parting words to me were, "Now it is your turn to see who is checking up on you." The phone never rang the rest of the day. I knew it wouldn't. I said it didn't matter, but it did. The truth is that no one knows or seems to care when I come and go but God.

That can be the reality for singles living alone and far from family. The reason may not be that their families don't care; it may be simply that they are not geographically near. Friends, too, may care, but often in an *ad hoc* way. In my case, friends may have called on that icy Friday night. Getting no answer, their assumption would have been that I was out of town, safely away from the storm. They probably would not try again.

The question remains: How do I deal with this isolation? I deal with it by giving my aching heart to Jesus because I believe he knows and deeply cares about me and my coming and going.

Like every other human being, I need to know I matter to someone. Sometimes that someone is seen only through the eyes of faith. As I face my feelings of isolation on the emotional level, and humbly turn to Jesus with them on the spiritual level, I have been given a deeper understanding and awareness of the mysterious oneness and sense of belonging that Jesus, and he alone, offers me.

He is *always* checking in on me, and he doesn't have to use the telephone. He is with me and within me. Jesus knows when I come and go because he comes and goes with me, always and everywhere.

Jesus draws me nearer to himself through my feelings of isolation. He also calls me to action. He encourages me to set aside my pride and openly express my feelings. Only by sharing my needs with others can I give people the opportunity to reach out to me in my times of need.

He calls me to be attentive to others, especially other singles who might be experiencing a similar sense of isolation. He asks me to make a phone ring in an apartment that might otherwise be silent. It might be in the midst of an ice storm, during a period of unemployment, or on a typical Sunday afternoon or Wednesday evening.

Isolation is part of the human experience Jesus felt as a man and overcame as the risen Son of God. He calls all of us — not just singles living alone or with roommates but also spouses, parents, or religious living in community — to face our feelings of isolation, not to deny them. He beckons us to share them with him. He understands. By comforting us with his understanding in the midst of our own aloneness, *he enables us* to reach out in empathy and love to others who may feel isolated too.

I am learning, slowly but surely, to accept my feelings of isolation. I can't say I like them, but I am experiencing how Jesus helps me grow through them. May we all be open to the oneness Jesus offers, especially in our moments of isolation.

No one else may know when we come and go — but, thank God, he does.

6

The Challenge
of Eating Alone

Do you struggle with your eating habits? Do you find it hard to eat alone? Do you catch yourself snacking when you are not even hungry?

My answer was yes to all of the above until I found a formula that worked for me — cole slaw, chili, chocolate milk, and Christ. Sound appetizing?

Actually, it is not the menu for one meal. Cole slaw is a favorite for lunch; a sandwich just doesn't taste the same without it. Chili is great for dinner on a cold winter Sunday, after smelling it simmer all afternoon. Chocolate milk, preferably lo-cal, is my way of satisfying my sweet tooth without splurging on another alliterative list of cravings like cookies, candy, and cake.

And Christ? He should really be first on the list since it is because of him and my "conversations" with him that I have taken that hard, often painfully honest look at myself and my eating habits. Through prayerful reflection and evaluation of how my single lifestyle affects my eating, I have learned to channel my habits into more healthy directions. The benefits have been both physical and spiritual.

Controlling my cravings and maintaining a regular meal schedule is a day-to-day challenge for me. Despite the great variety of diet and health-food books on the market, none of these popular solutions seemed to work for me.

It wasn't until I sat down and started asking myself tough questions — When do I eat? What do I eat? How do I eat? Why do I eat? — that I found the formula that helped me change my bad habits and establish good ones. By constantly turning to Christ for the discipline and strength to make the necessary changes, for the perseverance to stick with them, and for the forgiveness when I fail, I am happy to report I am winning the battle more often than I am losing it.

Much of what I discovered in my prayerful evaluation is directly related to being single. Because I lived alone and ate alone, I rarely made the effort to cook. Cooking for one person seemed extravagant. Consequently, I did not sit down to eat. Always on the run, I usually arrived home from work with only enough time to change my clothes and dash off to my evening activities.

I first consciously recognized this bad habit one night when, for some reason, I was home at a normal dinner hour and didn't know what to do with myself. I had time to cook, but there was nothing in the refrigerator — another bad habit. As the aroma of cooking filled the stairwell and seeped into my apartment, I was overwhelmed with the feeling of being left out. Not only did everyone else's dinner smell tantalizing but the sound of voices around their tables made me feel very alone. No wonder I was in the habit of working late. Admitting the reality of my situation brought forth the tears but, thankfully, prayers too.

That was the beginning of my change in habits. The very first thing I did was make a meal plan and grocery list. That may sound basic, but my cupboard was bare and I had to start from scratch. Guess what was on my list — cole slaw, chili, and chocolate milk. I decided one easy way to encourage myself to cook and eat at home was to prepare things I especially liked. What's more, I realized many meals can be made and frozen for future use. One pot of chili goes a long way for a single person.

Shopping and cooking were the easy steps. Learning to sit down and eat alone was the hard part. But that's where Christ came in. He gave me insight and practical ideas that have transformed the *act* of eating alone into an *experience* I now enjoy.

In fact, thanks to Christ, I do not eat alone. He is my guest, my family. I now make a point of setting the table for myself every evening with a cloth place mat, napkin, and lighted candle. These things once seemed frivolous to me when I thought of eating alone. Now when I think of serving a guest, my brother Christ, these details have meaning. No diet books ever advised this approach.

Music has also become an important part of my daily dining. It is relaxing to listen to classical music or my favorite spiritual albums as I eat. I compare it to the Mass. The Eucharist is sustenance for the soul with or without music. With musical accompaniment it seems much more beautiful. I have always found my sense of communion with the Lord encouraged through music. Adding it to the ''sacrament'' at the table in my home has enhanced my sense of Christ's presence during my solitary suppertimes.

But what about conversation? While it is one thing to know Christ is present, it is quite another to ''talk'' to him. I decided to try. I began by saying grace out loud, as I would if the table were surrounded with people joining me in prayer. Grace stretched into an ongoing prayer of thanks and petition, and I soon discovered praying during mealtimes was a very special way for me to converse with Christ. It was a time to thank him for my day and to bring him my concerns for family, friends, colleagues, and the world.

I feel a oneness with Christ through these conversations, and I see how he is also helping me turn my eyes away from myself and my aloneness and toward him and others. Have you ever noticed how close you feel to someone when you pray for that person? There may be no one sitting with me at my table, but I feel the presence of Jesus and the people for whom I pray.

Buying the right food, taking time to prepare it, and overcoming the obstacles of eating alone were crucial steps in the process of establishing good eating habits. But I still had a huge hurdle to jump — snacking. Again I had to ask: When do I snack and why?

I am most likely to look for something to munch when I am lonely, bored, under stress, or tired. At 10:00 P.M. when there is no one to hug good night, I take stock of what's in the refrigerator. When I am bored at work and the days seem long, I wonder what treat I can buy. When I am ''on the road'' for business and fatigue or tension erodes my self-discipline, I eat the dessert I should decline. And when I come home and there is no one to greet me but the cookie jar, you can guess what happens.

Snacking, and sweets in particular, are often more of an emotional craving than a physical one. That's probably why the struggle to curb those cravings is an ongoing one. It is also why I constantly turn to Christ, remembering, ''In him who is the source of my strength I have strength for everything'' (Philippians 4:13).

When the cravings come, I try to pray before immediately checking out the kitchen. I ask Christ to fill the voids in my heart that I am seeking to fill with a snack. I often put on my favorite spiritual songs to feed my soul instead of my body. I pass up dessert by remembering someone who is suffering and in need of my prayers. As small a sacrifice as it may seem, the conquering of my urge to snack becomes my prayer, and Christ once again coaxes me to look beyond myself.

I still nibble occasionally. I try to restrict myself to healthy items like fresh fruit and popcorn. I rarely fill the cookie jar or freezer with treats. Sometimes the sweet tooth does prevail, and a feeling of guilt follows close behind. At these times I have learned to appreciate Christ's infinite forgiveness. By accepting his forgiveness and forgiving myself, I admit my failure, forget it, and start again.

Thanks to Christ, I am making progress. I have regular and good eating habits most of the time. I am in better control of my cravings. My weight is stable. Most importantly, I have grown closer to Christ through the struggle.

Cole slaw, chili, and chocolate milk may temporarily satisfy my physical cravings. Yet, I know in my heart, my mind, and my body that Christ alone satisfies the hunger in my soul.

7

It's All
Up to Me

Sometimes life seems to be just one big "to do" list.

There is always laundry to do, groceries to buy, meals to prepare, buttons to replace, checkbooks to balance, oil to change, bills to pay, bathrooms to clean, gardens to weed. The list is endless.

My life is a list of "to dos" because some things just have to be done if I want to live responsibly. This list does not differ much from the ones my married or religious brothers and sisters have, except for one major factor: It's all up to me. There is no one with whom to share the burden of responsibility or to divide the chores of daily living.

The little "to dos" of life can get me down, especially since I have to be worried about the big things — like mortgage payments, furniture purchases, car repairs, a clogged bathtub, new business suits, and a book begging to be written. Sometimes overwhelmed, I am tempted to throw in the towel.

Sometimes the burden of it all hits hard, as on those days I pull the covers over my head and give in to the cold I have been fighting for weeks. Not only must I make my own chicken soup but also fetch my own aspirin and hot tea. Everything is up to me.

A single person, by necessity, must become a jack-of-all-trades — accountant, auto mechanic, gardener, errand-runner, plumber, dietician, nurse, investment advisor, chef, and seamstress. Single parents and singles caring for aging parents can probably add to this list. No wonder we feel heavily laden at times.

During such heavy-laden times, I have turned to Jesus for the relief he promises: "Come to me, all you who are weary and find life burdensome, and I will refresh you" (Matthew 11:28). He has given me the rest I needed and more.

Resting with Jesus, I have been refreshed and encouraged to reflect on my entire life and not just its burdens. He has lightened my load by filling my heart with gratitude. "It is good to give thanks to the LORD" (Psalm 92:2).

How thankful I become when I take time to share life's burdens with Jesus, for he shows me the blessings in the burdens. I have clothes to wash because I have clothes to wear. I have a mortgage to pay because I have a home to live in. I have meals to prepare because I have food to eat. I have money to spend or to save because I have a well-paying job. I have a car to fix because I have a car to drive. I have a book to write because I have a loving, growing, overflowing relationship with my Lord and Savior that I feel called to share with others.

How blessed I am. Our loving God has bestowed many gifts on me. Accepting these gifts means not only using them responsibly but also gratefully.

In addition to infusing my heart with his rest and spirit of thankfulness, Jesus gave me a new look at the order in my life. He taught me that my heaviness of heart was due, in part, to my own poor scheduling of activities. Too often I overbooked my calendar, leaving myself little or no time to do the laundry or balance the checkbook, much less shop and prepare meals in advance.

I realize I must put the laundry, the bank statements, and grocery shopping, to name a few, on my calendar as well as on my "to do" list. I must *schedule* the necessary time to complete these chores if I hope to reduce the tension created by doing them in a rush.

Jesus has also reminded me time and again that, while I shoulder the burdens of my life, I am not alone. It really isn't *all* up to me. He is always on hand to help, and so are others.

The responsibilities may indeed be all mine, but I need not *do* everything myself. In the office I delegate responsibilities that another person can do, often better than I can. Why not delegate my home responsibilities? My employer pays for this kind of arrangement at the office. Why not adjust my thinking and pay for such an arrangement in my home? Having reflected on these questions I now decide which tasks I will do and which ones I will delegate. I weigh the fee for service against the time and hassle necessary to do the task myself.

Some singles have a teenager clean their home. I prefer to do that myself, but I pay an accountant to do my taxes. Some like to tinker with their cars. I prefer to take my car to a reputable mechanic and "tinker" with the word processor. It is a matter of personal preference and budget.

There are some things that, due to money and time restraints, I choose not to do. Though I love flowers and would love to plant impatiens in front of my home, I am content merely to weed the garden and wait until next summer to plant. It would be nice to be a gourmet cook since I do enjoy cooking. But for now, because of my priorities and work schedule, I eat chili or a Stouffer's Lean Cuisine from my freezer.

It is up to me to decide. It is also up to me not to let the chores or societal pressures dictate my choices. For me, to decide, to make choices, means to pray. It means to follow Jesus' example and seek the Father's will in all facets of my life. Through prayer I have discovered that Jesus gives me rest, a grateful heart, and guidance. He gives me others to help me order the daily "to dos" of my life and to make major decisions.

Speaking of major decisions, Jesus has walked me through many of them, but his presence and guidance were dramatically apparent in my decision to buy a town house. The discernment process I went through in making this decision is my reason for sharing it with you.

Unfamiliar as I was with real estate and interest rates, I had never thought or even dreamed about buying a house. I always assumed that was done by married couples. Then one weekend, while visiting friends in North Carolina, I noticed myself periodically introducing real estate into the conversation. After this happened several times I decided to privately ask the Lord, "Are you trying to tell me something?"

Indeed he was. Initially I panicked — "I can't afford a house on a single income!" Recognizing I was too far from home to even begin investigating the financial aspects of such a decision, I settled for praying about what I would want to buy *if* I really could afford to buy. By the end of the weekend, God had given me an image of a two-story, one bedroom town house, with a small den, windows on three sides, and surrounded by trees.

Car-pooling with a friend on the first day back to work, I

exchanged pleasantries and then blurted out, "I think I am supposed to be buying a house." Her response was, "I know just the place." She was the first person God gave me to help me make this decision.

We looked at a condominium conversion project not far from where I lived. Wasn't I surprised to find myself looking at two-story town houses in many varieties, including some with a den, windows on three sides, and surrounded by trees.

In the two weeks that followed, a friend who is a real-estate agent drove me around to see other properties so I could shop and compare. Moreover, a longtime friend and "advisor" from New York and my sister and brother-in-law from Michigan visited. I was able to solicit their on-the-spot advice and reaction to my pending decision.

It was a hectic couple of weeks, compounded by my car literally dying and requiring a tow and many hundreds of dollars in repairs. Despite this financial drain, I continued to seek God's direction and the input of people he gave to assist me.

A mere three weeks from the day I had asked God if he wanted me to buy a house, I signed the purchase agreement on a town house that matched my Spirit-inspired image. If that wasn't enough to leave me in awe of Jesus' guidance, I became eligible for a special first-time buyer's mortgage interest rate. This rate was offered through the state on a first-come, first-served basis. I was informed of it mere moments before leaving on a five-day business trip. I made the necessary call from the airport to start the application process. Today I live in my dream house and pay a mortgage rate I will always consider to be manna from heaven.

In the daily "to dos" and major decisions of my life, I have learned to pray to Jesus every step of the way. Through his grace, I have seen the blessings in my burdens and have found ways to reorder my life so as to lighten the load. I have been gently guided through major decisions with the help of people Jesus knew I needed.

So that I may never forget the truth I have learned, I now have framed and prominently displayed in my bedroom the proverb: "In everything you do, put God first. He will direct you and crown your efforts with success."

8

I Think
I Need a Hug

She was only twelve, but my young friend was definitely in touch with her feelings. Arriving home from school one day, obviously distressed about something, she walked up to her mom and simply said, "I think I need a hug."

That may have been the first time I consciously recall hearing someone say it quite like that. Since then, I have read it in cartoons and little "hug books." I have heard speakers espouse it from the platform and on TV. Friends, family, and strangers seem willing to talk openly about it. It has even become popular to say, "I think I need a hug," and I am glad.

I am relieved because now I can say, "I think I need a hug," without being perceived as weak and dependent. I now feel more comfortable reminding people that singles especially need hugs since single life, by its very nature, does not lend itself to hugs on a daily basis.

Many times I have come home from work upset like my pre-teen friend, but with no one to hug me when I walked in the door. There has been no one to hug when I was excited about a job promotion, the publication of an article, or the birth of another niece, when I was sad about a movie I just watched or challenged by a book I was reading, when I missed my family or felt misunderstood by the world and in need of a caring touch.

We all have different reasons — in the past and in the present — for wanting and needing a hug. But for singles, and especially singles who live alone, hugs are often few and far between.

I am keenly aware of the lack of daily hugs because I grew up in what I affectionately call a "huggy-kissy" family. We hugged and kissed my parents good morning and good night. We kissed Dad before we jumped out of the car to go to school and kissed Mom when we came home every afternoon. One of the kids could often be seen sitting on the couch, as tots and teens, with my grandmother's arms around them. At times, we even hugged each other.

I was blessed with growing up in a family that loved each other and expressed this love openly with hugs and kisses. We continue to love and hug each other, and probably more openly and sincerely than we did as kids. I miss the affection, the support, the affirmation of daily hugs.

As a child I experienced hugs in a positive, growth-producing way. As a single adult I am now experiencing the lack of hugs in an equally positive, growth-producing way. While I still yearn for physical hugs and believe in the intrinsic value of a physical hug, I have come to appreciate the infinite varieties and value of non-physical hugs.

A letter in my mailbox, a long-distance phone call in the middle of the week, flowers delivered at the office, a card that signs off with "You're loved" — these are all wonderful hugs that fill my heart with the warmth I associate with a tender embrace or a big bear hug.

Some types of hugs are initiated by others, but there are also those initiated by me. Taking a moment to recall happy memories, sitting for hours captivated by photo albums filled with pictures of family and friends, or rereading old letters are just a few of the things I do when I think I need a hug.

Hugs come in many varieties if we are open to seeing and experiencing God's loving touch in our lives. Birds hopping across the windowsill . . . a sleeping baby in our arms . . . a clear, crisp morning . . . a snow-covered forest . . . the smell of brewed coffee . . . the crackle of a fire in the hearth . . . a look of understanding in the eyes of a friend . . . a toast of success — the list is endless.

Our loving Creator hugs as only he can. A cool breeze through an open window feels like a caress from God. A tree burning with the golden leaves of autumn or the delicate blossoms of a dogwood are his kisses. In the brilliance of a setting sun, or the striking contrast of the moon reflected on a midnight blue lake, I feel God's breathtaking embrace.

God's loving touch can also be felt in a sacramental sense. Whether I am listening to Christian music in the privacy of my home or singing with the community of believers in church, I am often moved to tears by the feelings of love that well up within me. Through all the sacraments, and regular sharing in Eucharist and Reconciliation, Jesus touches me.

Jesus has taught me much about the affection, the affirmation, the love communicated through hugs — all kinds of hugs. He has reminded me that to receive hugs is to give hugs. If I need a hug, it probably means I need to reach out and give a hug. Others need hugs too, and often can't verbalize this need as my pre-teen friend did.

As I reach out to hug and risk being rebuffed, I have learned to be sensitive to the feelings, the fears, the uncertainties, the comfort zones of others. I have learned to modify the hugs I give to adapt to a given situation or personality. A casual nudge to a co-worker can be as potent a touch as a heart-to-heart hug with a friend.

In a hug the act of giving and receiving can become one, provided both participants respond. This has special meaning for me, who wants so much to give hugs but often feels embarrassed to express my need to receive them. In one action my need to give and receive a hug is fulfilled.

Hugs took on even more significance for me when, one day in prayer, Jesus compared our relationship to a hug. Through nature, through music, through others, through the sacraments, Jesus embraces me and invites me to embrace him in return. Just as I know how much warmer any hug feels when it is mutual, I have come to appreciate how much deeper my relationship with Jesus is when I respond to him and hug him back.

Hugging Jesus means letting go of myself, my pride, my control, and allowing myself to enter fully into the mystery of God's love for me. It means thanking him for the blessings of life through which I feel his touch. It means sharing in the sacraments. It means believing in the goodness of myself and others. It means hugging others.

May we all grow in our appreciation and expression of hugs in our relationships with others and in our relationship with God. God the Father loves us so much that he sent his only Son to restore our relationship with him. His only Son loved us so much that he willingly stretched out his arms on a cross and embraced the world.

Now that's what I call a HUG!

9

It's Too Easy to Be Selfish

Sometimes it is hard to be single because it is just too easy to be selfish. My time is my own, my money is mine to spend as I will, my privacy is uninterrupted, and the noise in my home is controlled by me. There is no one needing me to fix a meal, wanting me to play with them, waiting for me to come home at night, or depending on my paycheck. My life is truly my own.

Because it is my own, because there is no one to draw me naturally out of myself, and nothing to force me to be there for another, I find that single life contains a real and insidious temptation to live a life of selfishness.

How easy it is to get caught up in my needs and desires, to worry about what I am to eat and wear, to focus on my pace, my travel schedule, my career, my need for hugs, my town house, my salary, my playtime. Even my prayer life is affected. I pray for the concerns of my family and friends, for the world and for our Church. Sometimes I forget somebody or something, but the list of petitions beginning with "my" is rarely forgotten.

In my tendency to be late, I have seen my self-centeredness and lack of consideration for others. Thinking twice before answering a hesitant "yes" when someone asks me a favor, I have put my concerns ahead of the concerns of others. In my relationships, I have been thoughtless, unforgiving, and hurtful, quick with a sarcastic comment or critical glance. And my checkbook shows who has been given top priority.

I struggle with the selfishness inherent in living alone. I struggle because part of me asserts, "I must take care of myself. I must look out for my career and my future. I must be aware of making time for fun as well as work because if I don't no one else will."

Even as I hear myself say these things, an inner voice reminds me that there is a fine line between self-fulfillment and selfishness, between self-confidence and pride, between self-knowledge and self-pity, between concern and worry.

How do I make the distinction between the healthy care for myself and the unhealthy concern that can lead to selfishness? How do I give of myself, yet maintain myself as only I can? How do I accept myself as the person God created me to be, yet constantly grow into the person he calls me to become? How do I search out the answers to these and other questions without falling victim to a thought process that revolves around me, myself, and I?

Jesus gave me the answers to these questions by painfully bringing my selfishness to my attention. I was working for a U.S. Congressman and answering his constituents' mail. The letters contained pleas for funding of programs for the poor, handicapped, homeless, underprivileged in this country and abroad. These letters raised my consciousness to the needs of people I had rarely been exposed to in my comfortable, middle-class existence. Despite what I read, I was still wrapped up in where my career was going, who I could find to accompany me on a trip to Ireland, what new furniture I would buy. How blinded, how selfish I was!

Then one night, as I was obsessed with one of my concerns, Jesus' love pierced my soul and revealed to me my "I-I-I" attitude. I was overcome with shame and sorrow. It hurt to take an honest look at myself. It was painful to acknowledge my selfishness. It saddened me to see how self-centered I had become. That night I became acutely aware of how hard it is to be single because it is so easy to be selfish.

Jesus did not leave me to wallow in my guilt. Praying "Lord Jesus Christ, Son of the Living God, have mercy on me a sinner," I begged for his forgiveness. I asked him to draw me out of myself and infuse me with his spirit of giving and self-denial. He reminded me of Saint Paul's words to the Galatians: " . . . Remember that you have been called to live in freedom — but not a freedom that gives free rein to the flesh. Out of love, place yourselves at one another's service. The whole law has found its fulfillment in this one saying: 'You shall love your neighbor as yourself' " (Galatians 5:13-14).

I repented of my selfishness and Jesus forgave me. In this

process I became aware of what I must do to resist the temptation of selfishness and to grow in my concern for others. Jesus instructed me to seek him constantly in the Scriptures, through the sacraments, and by serving others.

By reading and praying Scripture, I become more familiar with the Jesus who lived and died that I might know his Father's forgiveness. I am reminded of the wisdom of God, his precepts and commandments that teach me how to follow God's will and not my own.

Through Eucharist I relive Jesus' redemptive death and Resurrection and bow down before the God who gave so selflessly to me by allowing his Son to be crucified. In the sacrament of Penance (Reconciliation), I reach out like the woman who believed she would be healed if she just touched Jesus' cloak. Like that woman, I too experience the healing graces of forgiveness and renewal that come with confessing my selfishness before God.

By reaching out in loving service to others, I put their needs before mine. In little ways and big ways Jesus directs me to be mindful and helpful of others.

The newspapers are full of accounts of violence, oppression, starvation, discord. Now I pray the newspaper instead of just reading it. Contributing to hunger relief funds, shelters for the homeless, soup kitchens, and missionary efforts, I share my wealth with those who don't have the basics of life.

As I take time to visit the sick, the shut-in, and the forgotten in nursing homes, my own cares shrink in importance. Extending a helping hand to those faced with the responsibilities of an unwanted pregnancy or grief over the sudden death of a loved one, I offer support and strive to share Jesus' love and comfort.

Sometimes it is hard to be single because it is so easy to be selfish, but it is only by extending ourselves that we will experience the fullness of God's love.

"He who confers benefits will be amply enriched,
  and he who refreshes others will himself be refreshed."
(Proverbs 11:25)

Jesus confirms this in his teaching: " . . . In the measure you give you shall receive, and more besides. To those who have, more will be given; from those who have not, what little they have will be taken away'' (Mark 4:24-25).

If we seek Jesus in repentance, in Scripture, in sacraments, and in service, he will empower us with the will, the desire, and the ability to be selfless.

It is a constant battle, but Saint Paul encourages us as he encouraged the Galatians: '' . . . you should live in accord with the spirit and you will not yield to the cravings of the flesh'' (Galatians 5:16).

10

The Dating Scene Grows Old

At sixteen, my first date was an event. At twenty-four, my social life was a game. At thirty, untold dates and relationships later, the dating scene has grown old.

The nervousness of my youth gave way to young adult excitement of people to meet, places to go, and things to do. With that excitement also came a healthy dose of caution. While dating is often described as a game, it contains a certain amount of physical and emotional risk. I learned that in this game caution and calculated moves are as strategically important as in other games.

Filled with enthusiasm and armed with caution, I have dated. I have met dates in the laundromat and the grocery store, at the pool and the bus stop, on a blind date and on an airplane, framing pictures and jogging, through friends and politics. I have also answered personal "In Search Of" ads and have even tried my luck at computer dating. You name a way to meet a date, and I have done it. That includes the infamous "singles bars" and, on the opposite extreme, my parish Young Adults Club. To top all that, a man once handed me his business card at Lambert Airport in St. Louis. The card read: "I am looking for a wife. I am single. Please call."

I have been open to all possibilities in this dating game; and I have met neat people, visited interesting places, and done fun things. Let me add, I have also met my share of duds. I have played the game wholeheartedly. But, I admit, I am tired of "playing." The excitement has worn off, and I am weary of always calculating my moves.

I don't like my tendency to size up every man I meet, wondering: *Is he single? Christian? From a good family? Employed in a good job? Fond of children? Open and willing to share? Will we be compatible?* Those are but a few of the many questions that race through my mind whenever I meet someone to whom I feel attracted.

I am tired of playing because, as my questions indicate, I want to be serious. When I was looking for a "date," the questions used to be: Does he like to dance, play tennis, walk in the park, or visit museums? Those are the things I often did on dates. To play tennis with him, who needed to know if he liked children?

My questions have changed, as have the rules of the game. I am not just looking for a *date*. I am looking for a *mate*. The fun and frivolity of youth have been replaced by the goals and desires of a maturing adult. The rules have changed, and the "game" is more challenging. It was fun to date. It is hard to find a mate.

Finding a mate means first finding a date, then allowing a relationship to expand. Dining and dancing, playing tennis and visiting museums with a date lead to talking and sharing, meeting friends and family. Besides finding out if he likes children, finding a mate means learning whether the date has a personal sense of Jesus in his life. Building a relationship demands time, energy, emotion, and risk until it develops into a commitment. Sometimes this process from dating to relationship to permanent commitment is smooth. Many times it doesn't work that way.

This courting process could be compared to paying rent. Even after expending my time, energy, and emotion in a relationship, I often end up weeks, months, even years later with nothing to show for it. It is not until people make a commitment to each other that they begin to build equity in a relationship. I have paid my share of rent in relationships; I am ready to buy into a permanent commitment.

Sharing these feelings with others, I often have been misunderstood. People are quick to urge me to keep dating, as if I were going to stop. I know that dating is the first step in the process of mating. When others review ways for me to meet new people, I wonder how many times I must repeat, "I have tried that."

It is important for me to share with others my desire to meet that special someone because I never know whom they might know. But it is with Jesus that I share the depth of my feelings. It is with him that I am able to be completely honest. A priest reminded me of this one day in the confessional when he detected not just my frustration but also my misdirected anger. I had been caught in a web of self-pity that I thought came from feeling misunderstood by loved ones. In reality, I felt misunderstood by and angry toward God.

My penance that day was to sit down and tell Jesus exactly how I felt about my life. When I did, I discovered that I really wanted to follow his example and seek his Father's will in my life, but that I wasn't particularly pleased with his timing in revealing it to me. I felt I had been doing my part. When was God going to do his? I wasn't sitting home expecting "Mr. Right" to walk through my front door. I was out and about. What more could I do?

I heard Jesus say, as he has said to me many times, "Trust me." The benefits of trusting him were brought vividly to my attention shortly after I completed my tearful penance. I left one church and ended up at another for Saturday night Mass. Seated in front of me was a nice-looking man. Before the end of the evening, I had spent three hours in a nearby fast-food restaurant talking to him. We actually dated for a few months, but then our relationship ended. Despite its termination, I felt comforted in knowing Jesus had heard me. Meeting and dating this man gave me the positive reinforcement I needed to grow in my trust of Jesus in the dating game.

Meanwhile, I am trusting Jesus and doing things differently from what most people would recommend. Last year I committed myself and my time to a team of ten women preparing and giving a women's Cursillo retreat. By the world's standards, this is an unlikely place to meet a potential date. But God tells us in the words of Isaiah the prophet:

" . . . my thoughts are not your thoughts,
nor are your ways my ways, says the LORD."
(Isaiah 55:8)

Listening to Isaiah we learn that God's ways are mysterious. Isaiah also encourages us to trust in the Lord and search for his presence in our lives when he says:

"Seek the LORD while he may be found . . . "
(Isaiah 55:6)

Seeking the Lord, I answered his call to serve on the Cursillo team. In the weeks immediately following the retreat, I had dates with four different men.

One man, whom I had met four months earlier, called and asked me out for a pizza. Another, whom I had met at the pool months earlier, literally bumped into me at the produce counter in the grocery store. We later went to a movie together. The third was visiting Washington, DC, from North Carolina; mutual friends from Chicago had suggested he call me. Still another lived in my neighborhood and was looking for an ice-skating partner.

Through these events I learned a vital lesson about the dating game that has given me new energy and peace in this game and in the game of life. It wasn't what I did to find a date that produced these opportunities but what God did for me because I sought him and his ways. I was overwhelmed with God's faithfulness to me.

As Christians, we have a choice. We can play the games of life by Jesus' rules and "ways" or by the world's. As for me, I choose to trust him.

11

Sex and
the Single Christian

Sex and the single Christian. Talk about opening "Pandora's Box"!

As much as I wanted to skip this chapter, I knew I couldn't. I have received letters from readers pleading that someone address the subject of sex from a Christian perspective. One reader wrote: "Sex is where single Christians are really in the 'Twilight Zone.' I have so much confusion and conflict in this area that I can't begin to sort it out. I'd like to say that sex outside of marriage is a sin, pure and simple, but current thought won't let me. I often wonder if I am normal."

As single Christians in today's society, we do experience much confusion and conflict when it comes to sorting out our sexual feelings and actions. Following Jesus, striving to live according to his Word, sets us apart from those caught up in the current, pervasive "free sex" attitudes and trends. We wonder, "Am I normal?"

We live in a society that seems to accept, even condone, any and all expressions of sexual desire whenever, however, and with whomever it may be excited. Sex can be as casual as a one-night stand, as planned as an unmarried couple living together, or as base as prostitution.

We can watch it on TV, purchase it from behind the cash register at the local drugstore, and feature it as entertainment at a party. We can do it with those of the opposite sex, same sex, or both, whatever our inclination. We can do it in groups or alone. Many people can and do elevate it to its fullest potential within the sacred bonds of marriage. Others, albeit few in number, choose to abstain from it because of vocation or personal conviction. We can choose from such a mixed bag these days!

Where do Christian singles fit into this scenario? Are there no rights and wrongs anymore? Is it really OK to do it just because it feels good? The world doesn't seem to acknowledge anything as immoral or illicit. Does Jesus? What insight does the Word of God give us as we try to sort out the answers to these questions *for ourselves?*

I emphasize seeking the answers *for ourselves* because I feel the subject of sex is one of the most private and most mysterious areas of our lives. Aside from my relationship with God, there is nothing more private, more mysterious, and perhaps more frightening than discovering my sexuality and how to express it as the single Christian I claim to be.

By today's standards I am what many people call a "prude." Since I was a teenager I have believed and internalized the attitude that sex between two people who are not married to each other is forbidden in the eyes of God. This attitude has been tested time and again by my own sex drive and desire, by dates, peers, and Christian friends. Challenged by Christians — the very people I had assumed shared my attitude because they shared my faith — I became confused. Most of my confusion stemmed from the fact that I didn't have the scriptural knowledge at my fingertips to validate my "prudish beliefs" for myself, much less for others.

Turning to Scripture, I read passages from Genesis (39:6-10), Leviticus (18:22-23), Proverbs (7:15-27), Ecclesiastes (3:1-8), Ezekiel (23:13-17), 1 Corinthians (6:9-10,16,18), Ephesians (4:17-24, 5:3-7), Hebrews (13:4), and Revelation (2:20-21). God revealed his wisdom and commandments to me through these books of the Old and New Testaments, but I continued my search. I wanted to find the truth as spoken by Jesus.

A friend directed me to the Gospels of Mark and Matthew and what I now understand to be Jesus' teaching on sex and the single Christian. In Mark 7:21-23, Jesus says: "Wicked designs come from the deep recesses of the heart: acts of fornication, theft, murder, adulterous conduct, greed, maliciousness, deceit, sensuality, envy, blasphemy, arrogance, an obtuse spirit. All these evils come from within and render a man impure." Another version of this teaching also appears in Matthew 15:19-20. In both places Jesus refers to fornication and adultery as evils, as sins, impure acts.

Fornication is sexual intercourse between two unmarried people. Adultery is sexual intercourse between two people, at least one of whom is married to someone else. If we accept these definitions of fornication and adultery, and accept Jesus' teaching about them, then Jesus is saying that premarital sex, affairs, "flings," prostitution, and homosexual relations are impure acts.

Continuing my Scripture search, I found Saint Paul's teaching to the Corinthians, which opened my eyes even more. In 1 Corinthians 6:9-10, Paul writes: "Do not deceive yourselves: no fornicators, idolaters, or adulterers, no [sexual perverts] thieves, misers, or drunkards, no slanderers or robbers will inherit God's kingdom."

If we hope to inherit God's kingdom, then we must acknowledge God's Word about fornication and adultery. If we don't, will we be any different from the Pharisees whom Jesus criticized?

"You hypocrites! How accurately did Isaiah prophesy about you when he said:
'This people pays me lip service
but their heart is far from me.
They do me empty reverence,
making dogmas out of human precepts.' "
(Matthew 15:7-9)

If we sincerely want to follow our Lord, then we must turn to him for the courage and conviction, the self-control and discipline to deal with the sexual feelings within us and the daily pressures around us as we live a life of chastity. We must seek him with a contrite heart and beg his forgiveness for our failings and sins of the past. We need to pray:

"Your ways, O LORD, make known to me;
teach me your paths.
Guide me in your truth and teach me,
for you are God my savior,
and for you I wait all the day.

Remember that your compassion, O LORD,
   and your kindness are from of old.
The sins of my youth and my frailties remember not;
   in your kindness remember me,
   because of your goodness, O LORD.'' (Psalm 25:4-7)

I have prayed for the strength of mind and body to obey God's Word about sex, and Jesus has enlightened me. I am working through the misconceptions and guilt of my youth because I can now accept my sexual desire as the good and natural instinct God created in me. I no longer feel guilty merely because I feel this drive and experience frustration because I choose not to consummate it.

Jesus has directed me to adhere to a regular exercise program in order to release the tension, to expend pent-up energy, and to experience the relaxation that follows physical exertion. I have gained a new appreciation of the sport of swimming. When I was a competitive swimmer in college, the water was my adversary. These days when I work out, I appreciate the water's caress as I swim. When I let my exercise routine slip, my sex drive becomes more difficult to control.

I have learned to avoid those things that are sexually stimulating. I hear the wisdom in Saint Paul's First Letter to the Thessalonians: ''It is God's will that you grow in holiness: that you abstain from immorality, each of you guarding his member in sanctity and honor, not in passionate desire as do the Gentiles who know not God'' (1 Thessalonians 4:3-5).

I carefully select the movies I watch, books I read, magazines I buy, and parties I attend. I refuse to watch soap operas and won't engage in conversation about them. People make fun of me for my prudish choices, but I consider them *prudent*. I just don't need to excite feelings that cannot be fulfilled. Rather, I choose sanctity, honor, and God's will over my passionate desire.

'' . . . I will walk in the integrity of my heart,
   within my house;
I will not set before my eyes
   any base thing. . . . ''
(Psalm 101:2-3)

51

I think of my prudence as a form of dieting. If I want to be thin, I avoid sweets. If I want to be holy, I avoid sin. To reduce the temptation to snack, I don't buy cookies and ice cream. Similarly, I avoid sexually explicit movies and novels to reduce the temptation to commit sexual sin. I decline the sexual advances of a date because it is too hard to eat just one potato chip and stop.

While exercising and avoiding temptation are practical ways of building self-control and discipline, I still must fight the inner battle. I must pray constantly because I hunger for the sweetness of a kiss, the passion of an embrace, the ecstasy of intercourse, the warmth of a man sleeping next to me. Alone and in the dark of night, it is difficult. In love with someone, it is a heartrending physical and emotional struggle.

Daily I must submit my mind and body to the will of God. I must place my relationships in God's hands. I must avoid situations that could put me in a compromising position. I must deny myself and pick up the cross of chastity because I have chosen to follow Jesus, who said: "Whoever wishes to be my follower must deny his very self, take up his cross each day, and follow in my steps" (Luke 9:23).

I must also repent and ask for God's forgiveness and for the willpower to start again when I falter in carrying this cross, knowing that:

"He who conceals his sins prospers not,
    but he who confesses and forsakes them obtains mercy."
(Proverbs 28:13)

Obedience does reap benefits. I live with an inner peace. I am not afraid of being used, abused, or infected with one of the diseases transmitted through promiscuity. I have no anxiety about becoming pregnant because abstinence is still the most reliable and risk-free form of birth control.

In my dating relationships I make it clear, and usually at the beginning, what my beliefs are. I take the risk of being rejected on the basis of my convictions. I have learned it is easier to discern the potential, the depth or the lack of it, in my relationships when sex is not allowed to be the driving force.

I am careful about the signals I give so as not to mislead or hurt the men I date. It is difficult to balance this caution with the freedom to be the affectionate, sexual person that I am and want to communicate to a man. Through such balancing acts, I have learned the value of dating men who share my understanding of Jesus' teachings about sex. When we each hold the same convictions, it becomes a shared responsibility to keep our sexual relationship in check.

By rechanneling my physical energies and tension as I abstain, I control my sex drive instead of it controlling me. This self-control will bear fruit if and when I do marry. Marriage includes sex, but it also restricts it. There will be times during married life when it will be necessary to refrain from sexual intercourse. Single chastity is good practice for marital fidelity.

There is heavy emphasis today on sexual technique and prowess, on making sure two people are sexually compatible before they marry. I agree that sexual compatibility is important in marriage, but I believe that the most important technique to master before marriage is open, honest communication, not sexual gymnastics.

Compatibility in marriage hinges on a couple's ability to communicate. If two people can talk and work out their preferences and their differences, and if both partners sincerely and willingly submit their hearts and bodies to God so as to seek his direction in their relationship, then the sexual techniques and compatibility will fall into proper place with pleasure and peace.

The fruit of marriage — sexual intimacy — must ripen in an environment of trust, commitment, security, and love. If this fruit is left on the tree during the courtship, then it will be healthy and delicious when it is picked after marriage. Despite popular opinion to the contrary, I am trusting God that this is true.

Chastity also reaps everlasting good. Through chastity and the struggle to live it, I am drawn closer to Jesus. As Christians, we know that the pain of the Cross led to the joy of the Resurrection. Jesus promises that when we carry our crosses, trusting in him and his Father's will, we too will enjoy his victory. He will draw us closer to himself and his Father and give us his Spirit of peace and joy as we persevere in obedience.

With God's grace I shall persevere. Bound by my vows of

Baptism, which profess allegiance to Jesus and rejection of Satan and all his works, I shall strive to live a life of holiness regardless of what the world condones. By the love of Jesus and the self-discipline and self-control he alone can nurture within me, I will continue to say "No" even when my body aches to say "Yes."

I am inspired to carry on this fight with my flesh by the example of Saint Francis of Assisi. Saint Francis is said to have thrown himself into a rose garden in repentance for his sins of the flesh. Legend says that the Lord spared him, that the thorns disappeared.

It was while visiting Assisi and gazing at a garden of rosebushes that I heard this story for the first time. The priest who told it to me later commented that when he chooses some kind of self-denial, like fasting or abstinence, to overcome his passions, he has noticed how often the pain disappears. He experiences the wonderfulness of God and the joy of intimacy with his Lord.

As single Christians sorting out our sexual feelings, experiences, dreams, and desires, we must constantly strive to follow our Lord by remembering: " . . . the body is not for immorality; it is for the Lord, and the Lord is for the body. God, who raised up the Lord, will raise us also by his power" (1 Corinthians 6:13-14).

By the Lord's power and our obedience to his Word, the thorns of chastity will be removed; and he will raise us up in joy and peace, now and forever.

12

Feelings for Someone Who Is Unavailable

I have seen the look and felt the pangs. The look is one of sadness, confusion, and pain. The pangs pierce the heart that wants to deny the reality and be fulfilled despite the consequences.

What am I describing? You will know if you have ever experienced that heavy feeling in your chest when you realized you had feelings for someone who was unavailable or that an unavailable person had feelings for you. With that realization comes a painful moment of reckoning — "What am I to do?"

I have been there, and so have many of my friends and acquaintances. I have met few people who haven't been there to some degree or another. Despite the extreme sensitivity I touch within myself and in others, I feel called to discuss this subject.

We are talking about the heart. The heart is vulnerable because the heart is guided by feelings. Feelings don't always want to abide by the laws of God.

That is why a woman finds herself in love with her professor or a man with his secretary. Or why a nun falls in love with a priest she works with, or a seminarian with a woman he is counseling. Or why two people who once had been in love find out years later that they still love each other but are married to other people. That is why single people fall in love with married people and married people with single people.

Novels, movies, magazines, and soap operas are full of stories of people with feelings for those who are unavailable. What is sad is that we rarely are exposed to the stories of people learning to live with unrequited love. Our national attention seems to be focused on the intrigue, gossip, and havoc created by requited love between those who are unavailable. Prime-time television and personal advertisements soliciting "discreet relationships" attest to society's eroding standards of morality.

We Christians are not exempt from finding ourselves in love with people who are unavailable. We also are not exempt from the longing to let our feelings go and fulfill our fantasies. The question for us, as believers in Jesus and the laws of his Father, is: What are we to do with our feelings for those who are unavailable?

First, we accept them for what they are — feelings. In themselves, feelings are neither right nor wrong. They may consist of a tickle to the heart, an infatuation, or an intense love and devotion. They may well up from within when we least expect them. Wherever they fall within this spectrum, feelings are real and must be acknowledged and addressed.

The tendency may be to run, to avoid, to ignore, to deny. Unfortunately, fast as we may run, evasive tactics rarely erase such feelings. They may be submerged for a time, but if buried indefinitely they are likely to reemerge when we may be less able to control them.

Let's face it. It hurts to acknowledge something or someone we want and cannot have. It seems easier to pretend that we really don't have these feelings, that this isn't happening to us, that if we ignore them they'll go away. The ways of the world tempt us with: "Go with the flow" and "If it feels good, do it." We agonize. Confusion clouds our minds and torments our souls. Where can our hearts find peace?

Our hearts can find peace only through Jesus and the Spirit of courage, wisdom, discipline, and love Jesus gives us.

I have turned to Jesus when I discovered my feelings for someone who was unavailable and when an unavailable someone expressed his feelings toward me. With Jesus I have found the courage to stop running and to honestly face my feelings and the situation. He has given me the wisdom to see things as they really are and not as I would want them to be. He has empowered me with the discipline to live according to his laws, despite the pain in my heart, and the discipline to follow his Father's will rather than my own. Jesus has loved me in my weakness and filled the voids in my heart as only he can fill them. He has used all of these experiences to teach me about the mystery of love, about myself, about my relationship with others, and about my relationship with him.

I have come to understand and accept the nature of feelings — there is no right and wrong in the heart. It is natural to feel attraction and love for another. What we must remember is that while God does not judge our feelings as right or wrong, he does judge our actions.

Society's tacit approval of affairs does not make them right or good. Acting out feelings for someone who is unavailable, as sincere and deep as these feelings may be, is not God's way. We believe in the God who commands, "You shall not commit adultery" (Exodus 20:14). We believe in the God who outlines for us what will be judged as wrong.

To be true to our God and to ourselves, we must not act out our feelings for someone who is unavailable. To do so would be to sin. Sin estranges us from God and brings pain and turmoil into our lives and the lives of those we love. However, the question remains: What are we to do?

We are to blow out the match before it ignites a flaming passion. For many it means ending a relationship. For others it means placing strict controls on it. For some it means loving through silence and prayer. For most it means minimizing contact with the unavailable person. It means turning to God in our emptiness and sadness as we let go of our feelings for someone who is unavailable. God's wisdom tells us: When we play with fire we risk getting burned. It is far easier to blow out a match flame than to put out a forest fire.

Another analogy also makes the point. A friend once compared his feelings to a hand in a card game. Someone dealt him the cards. He couldn't explain why; he just knew he had them. He wanted to play the cards — act out his feelings for an unavailable woman — and he was trying to justify his actions. He felt that because he was given his feelings by someone beyond himself — a someone he could not identify — it must be acceptable to act upon them.

I thought about this image of cards for a while, and Jesus gave me his way of looking at it. Someone whom I call God deals the hand of life. Just as God gave Adam and Eve the Tree of Life, he also gave them the freedom to choose whether or not to obey his commands regarding that tree.

God has dealt me a hand of feelings. At times this hand has included feelings for someone who was unavailable. God also gave me the freedom to choose to play this hand according to the winning game plan of his commandments. As in any card game, winning sometimes means holding or discarding a card or two — never playing them. It may even mean folding the entire hand and starting over. The trump card in this game is my freedom to choose. It is up to me, and only me, to use this card judiciously.

It is not easy. In fact, for us singles it may be especially difficult because we don't have a spouse who is the object of our affection and vice versa. Because we hunger for this mutual affection, our feelings can be easily misdirected. What's worse, sometimes it seems that unavailable people see singles as ''open game,'' unattached and therefore available. No one can deny the temptation around us and the weakness within us.

Let's turn to Jesus for the strength to resist temptation, to endure the pain, and to trust the wisdom and promise in his Father's commandments. And if we fail, let's also remember the forgiving, understanding Jesus who said to the adulteress in John's Gospel, ''Nor do I condemn you. You may go. But from now on, avoid this sin'' (John 8:11).

Feelings will be feelings. Actions will be actions. We hold the match. We hold the hand of cards. It is our choice to blow out the match, to discard, or to take whatever action is necessary to live according to God's commandments.

PART TWO

GROWING
IN MY
RELATIONSHIP
WITH JESUS

13

Learning
to Pray

Something happened. I am not sure exactly what or how, but something happened to open my eyes to my relationship with Jesus and my need to grow in it through prayer.

God has always been a part of my life. I grew up in a loving, religious family and attended Catholic grade school and high school. During my college years, when many of my peers were lax about church, I continued to attend Sunday Mass regularly. I prayed alone, but sporadically, usually right before exams. Basically I knew God was near when I needed him, but I tended to forget about him from Sunday to Sunday when life was smooth and easy.

When I moved to a big city to launch my career and live the single, independent life, my attitude began to change slowly. Something spurred me into taking a new look at my relationship with God.

Was it because of my involvement in the Young Adults Group in the neighborhood parish I joined? Was it my ongoing conversation with my sister and brother-in-law, who had joined a covenant charismatic community? Was it because I was listening more intently to the Sunday Scripture readings or becoming personally acquainted with the young priests at the parish? Was it because I needed God to help me write the monthly editorials my new job required? Or did all of these factors together comprise the something that happened in my relationship with God?

I may never be able to answer these questions, but I do know something happened because I became aware that God wasn't just a peripheral part of my life. Rather, Jesus, by his life, death, and Resurrection, was inviting me to be in relationship with him, and through him to know his Father and receive the Holy Spirit. What a revelation that was! Jesus was asking me to be his friend.

My friendship with Jesus was not easy at first. I struggled with calling him by name. Having always prayed formally to God, I initially felt uncomfortable speaking on a casual, first-name basis to Jesus. But I learned.

As I learned, I found my desire to spend time with my newfound friend increasing. I began to attend daily Mass sporadically and read the Bible before falling asleep at night. Whenever I saw my sister and brother-in-law, we always seemed to talk about Jesus. Within me I felt stirrings I could not identify, and I wasn't sure what to do about them.

Then one particular Epiphany Sunday, when a Jesuit priest friend directed his homily *to me,* I began to understand. We had been out to lunch the day before, and I had tried to explain to him what I was feeling. I don't remember what he said to me over lunch, but I will never forget his homily that Sunday. His message was simply that we are like the three kings who, upon encountering Jesus, had to take another route home.

Thanks to my friend's homily, I identified those mysterious stirrings within me as my encounter with Jesus. Jesus was obviously inviting me to grow closer to him, to change my course, and to take another route home to him. So, I began to explore in new directions.

I took part in a Life in the Spirit seminar and participated in a charismatic prayer group for a short time. Then I moved. In my new location I was near several Catholic universities, so I enrolled in continuing education classes in theology and spirituality. I participated in a parish renewal program and a Cursillo weekend. On that weekend I met a Cenacle Sister, who introduced me to the concept of ongoing spiritual direction and suggested I call her if I wanted to pursue it. I called. Under her direction I began to pray alone on a regular basis.

It wasn't until I decided to devote time each day to sitting with Jesus in prayer that I discovered how special, how deep, how infinite, how comforting, how revealing, and how intimate my relationship with him could be. I started out slowly, but quickly picked up speed. The more time I spent with Jesus, the closer I felt to him and the more time I wanted to spend with him.

In the beginning, I was lucky to sit down for five minutes before dashing off to work. Then it was twenty minutes. I would read a short passage from Scripture and close my eyes and picture myself in the scene. Later, I decided to pray the annotated version of the *Spiritual Exercises* of Saint Ignatius and devoted an hour a day to Jesus in prayer for the next nine months. These exercises helped me establish a regular and comfortable prayer routine. Because of them I had weekly consultations with my spiritual director. In time I began to explore centering prayer. Asking Jesus to empty my mind of all thoughts and images, I sat quietly waiting for Jesus to fill me with his love and presence.

My relationship with Jesus has continued to grow as I continue to pray. Through prayer I have been drawn closer to Jesus as my friend, my Savior, my personal contact with God the Father and the Holy Spirit within me. I have come to understand myself better. I have felt the unconditional love the triune God has for me despite how sinful, weak, and incomplete I am. Because of Jesus I have experienced the forgiveness and redemption that empowers me to keep trying and to become all that his Father created me to be.

With every question Jesus answers for me in prayer, he gives me another to ponder. Thus our relationship knows no bounds. He daily calls me to see him in every person and every situation in my life. He helps me look at my single life, with all its joys and challenges, through his eyes. How different my life looks and feels seen through the eyes of Jesus and shared intimately with him as friend.

I encourage anyone searching for a deeper awareness of Jesus' presence to take time to pray. Do whatever is comfortable. Just begin. Let Jesus take the lead.

Don't be afraid to explore new paths, new styles of prayer. There is formal and spontaneous prayer, imaging with Scriptures, and writing in a journal. There is silent prayer and prayer through song and the mysterious gift of tongues. It is important to pray alone, but it is also important to pray with others in small, intimate groups and in the larger community at church.

We may pray with hearts full of praise and thanksgiving at times or with hearts heavily laden with repentance and petition. Sometimes our prayer may be flowing and freeing; at other times it may feel dry and lifeless. Prayer will be peaceful and comforting, but it also can be challenging and difficult. One way to sift through prayer experiences is to share them with a spiritual director.

Even as I describe prayer as I have experienced it with Jesus, I find I am using words that could describe the ups and downs of any relationship in my life. Prayer is the way I relate to Jesus. Sometimes we are on; sometimes we are off. But one thing I know for sure: He is with me always, no matter how I may feel about him or the situation at a given moment.

Something definitely happened to me when I realized I had met Jesus, when I realized he was inviting me not just to gaze at him in the manger or on the Cross but to relate to him as friend. And something really happened to me when I discovered how to relate to him through prayer.

Encountering Jesus means taking another route home. The first step on that journey is learning to pray.

14

Coping
with Loneliness

For me, loneliness comes and goes. It can be a fleeting moment of
wishing there were someone to chat with or a sustained pain of
missing a loved one who is far away. The emptiness and isolation I
feel when I am lonely can be so uncomfortable that I have often run
from it and pretended it really didn't exist.

My ways of coping with loneliness in the past have been to turn
on the radio, pick up the phone, or fill my schedule with lots of
people to see and places to go. Sometimes my calendar has been so
booked that the little time I had at home was filled with the chores
at hand.

Despite how busy I was and how fast I ran, I never outran
loneliness. It would always catch up with me at some point. I
would notice the times I ate alone, came and went with no one
knowing. I would miss family and friends, near and far, and be
hurt by the silent phone and empty mailbox. I would catch myself
falling into the trap of self-pity.

I first came to grips with my loneliness a few years ago when I
discovered how frenetic my lifestyle had become. My days were
full of constant activity, my home with constant noise, despite the
fact that I lived alone. My mind was full of clutter. I raced from
person to place and from place to person, boastfully claiming how
content I was but feeling fragmented and lonely inside.

Eventually, this lifestyle caught up with me. I became both
physically and emotionally exhausted. I was forced to slow down,
to sleep, to spend time alone just to catch my breath. It didn't take
too many evenings at home alone to bring forth the tears and the
prayers.

The tears came as I allowed myself to feel the pain and longing in the depths of my heart and soul. The prayers came as I cried out to the Lord:

"Look toward me, and have pity on me,
   for I am alone and afflicted.
Relieve the troubles of my heart,
   and bring me out of my distress."
(Psalm 25:16-17)

The Lord brought me out of my distress by first helping me identify the source of my loneliness. He helped me get in touch with the needs and desires in my life that went unnoticed or unfulfilled. He taught me which of these needs and desires were part of being human, living in an imperfect world, and which ones were results of my self-centeredness and unrealistic expectations of others.

I am lonely when I don't *feel* loved. I know family and friends love me, but I don't always feel their love. When I write letters to my family and receive no response for months, I don't feel their love. Friends love me, but I wonder if they think of me. When I call my married friends I often hear them say, "Come over anytime." Rarely do I hear, "Please join us today, tomorrow, or next week." The first statement leaves it all up to me; the second specifically invites and says, "You're loved, and we want you to be with us." I hunger to feel that.

I need not be alone to feel alone. Sometimes I am lonely in a crowd. Small talk and role-playing contribute to the indifference and distance I associate with loneliness. I have experienced this especially when I travel on business. After a full day of interaction with business associates, I can still feel quite empty. Then I must retire to an impersonal hotel room and the companionship of the television. Often when I have tried to fill the void by calling a loved one, I have been foiled by a busy signal or no answer.

I feel lonely because of a lack of intimacy in my relationships with others. Transient relationships seem to dominate the single lifestyle. People come and go in my life, leaving little opportunity to build gradually the trust that invites people to grow closer and take the risk of revealing themselves to me and myself to them.

Dating is a "here today, gone tomorrow" scene. Friends marry and often have little time for their single peers. Singles move from city to city. It is hard to interweave my life emotionally or physically with the lives of others like myself who are constantly on the move.

I yearn for more intimacy in my relationships with family and close friends. I feel frustrated and hurt when someone I love doesn't feel the need or desire to grow closer to me. The pangs of loneliness have stabbed deeply through the detachment and rejection I have felt from those I love and those I was counting on to love me.

One of my most painful experiences with loneliness came after a long-distance conversation with my parents. I had written them a letter in which I had bared my soul and shared some deep feelings. I must have been expecting some kind of affirmation from them, but they did not respond. When I finally asked them about my letter their indifferent response crushed me. Hearing "I can't quite remember what it said," I felt rejected. I felt misunderstood and unloved. Blinded by hurt, I found it hard to forgive. I found it hard to pray. Consequently, I couldn't feel God's love either.

In this state of brokenness I participated in a Cursillo retreat as a candidate. During a quiet time in the chapel on the first night, I closed my eyes and saw an image of Jesus walking hand in hand with me on a path. I was tightly gripping his hand, afraid he would let mine go. Over the course of the retreat I was affirmed out of my brokenness as my own high level of expectation and lack of forgiveness were revealed to me. I experienced the love of Christian community as never before, and my image of walking with Jesus changed.

By the end of the weekend my grip relaxed as I once again felt Jesus' love and forgiveness and the love of others. That weekend I learned that Jesus' hand is always extended to me. I need only take it, hold it, and trust him as my constant companion on life's journey.

My Cursillo experience dramatically changed my life, my faith, my concept of Christian community, and my ways of coping with loneliness. Since that weekend, the image with Jesus has appeared to me many times during prayer. We have been known to stop on the path and embrace. I have sat at his feet. I have cried on his shoulder. He has pointed something out to me in the forest ahead of us, laughed with me at the silly things I have done, paused to cherish a precious moment when our path crossed the path of another, and waited for me to repent the sins I have committed.

Through these descriptive, comforting images Jesus has taught me that he is indeed with me, always and everywhere. When I need to be reassured of this or need to *feel* his love and presence, his security and strength, I close my eyes and imagine my hand in his.

"Yet with you I shall always be;
  you have hold of my right hand;
With your counsel you guide me,
  and in the end you will receive me in glory."
(Psalm 73:23-24)

Through the prayer experiences that have arisen from my loneliness, I have learned why I am lonely. I have accepted my need to be loved as the basic human need that it is and not as a sign of weakness. I have learned that my yearning for intimacy is also normal — but that I sometimes have unreasonable expectations of my family and friends. Being so caught up in my own needs, I have failed to notice that others' needs for intimacy are different from mine.

My heart had to accept what my head already knew: that no one person can ever take away my loneliness. That's up to God. Moreover, God's love is constant and ever-present whether I feel it or not. I now know that when I don't feel his love it is usually because I have let go of Jesus' hand, not because he has withdrawn his from mine.

Now when I feel the pangs of loneliness, I turn to Jesus and squeeze his hand. He helps me to identify and express why I am lonely and then to cope with my loneliness in constructive and healthy ways.

Many lonely people seek solace in food, alcohol, drugs, and sex. My constant Companion and Teacher says to me, "Turn to me in the Scriptures and in prayer." Many devote excessive time to work and study. Jesus instructs me, "Spend time with the disadvantaged, the sick, the elderly, and relieve their loneliness." Many lose themselves in cults or in fictional lives on TV and in novels. Jesus calls to me: "Lose yourself in me, and you will find yourself."

Many feel forgotten by the Christian community and become resentful. Jesus reminds me, "Persevere and nurture my Church through prayer groups, service, and ongoing involvement in your parish and Cursillo communities." Many rush around in avoidance. Jesus says to me, "Be still and know that I am God." When I am alone and quiet, Jesus invites me, "Share your solitude with me, and I will make it solitary splendor."

More than once Jesus has transformed my loneliness into solitary splendor. I now appreciate and seek stillness. I strive to follow the example Jesus set: "Rising early the next morning, he went off to a lonely place in the desert; there he was absorbed in prayer" (Mark 1:35). I spend daily quiet times in prayer in my Lazy-Boy chair and evenings of reflection in my bedroom. I attend daily Mass and receive the Eucharist as often as possible. I take self-directed retreat weekends in my home or in a secluded cabin at the beach.

When I find myself dashing from activity to activity, I stop myself by repeating, *"Be still and know that I am God."* I turn off the TV at home and the radio in the car. I ask Jesus to give me his grace of solitary splendor so that I may grow closer to him, more trusting of his grasp of my hand, and more willing to give my love unconditionally to others.

Loneliness undoubtedly will continue to come and go. Coping with it now means first identifying the unmet needs that create it, then presenting them to God as we are instructed to do in Saint Paul's Letter to the Philippians: " . . . Present your needs to God in every form of prayer and in petitions full of gratitude. Then God's own peace, which is beyond all understanding, will stand guard over your hearts and minds, in Christ Jesus" (Philippians 4:6-7).

God's own peace stands guard over my heart because I now know and trust that Jesus is holding my hand.

15

On the Job

Flipping hamburgers at the local Burger King was my first real job. Not only was it a thrill for me as a teenager to have a job but it meant the more hours I worked the more hours of figure-skating lessons I could take. Besides, it was fun working with my friends.

Work took on new meaning when I decided to go to college. It didn't matter what the job was as long as it paid. I was short-order cook at the K-Mart grill, dental assistant in my dad's office, cleaning lady for any and all clients I could find, swimming teacher and lifeguard at the local pools. My skating lessons paid off, because teaching skating in the recreation program at five dollars an hour was a substantial supplement to my meager college funds.

Work took on still greater meaning when, armed with a bachelor's degree in history from the University of Michigan, I searched for a job, preferably something in communications/public relations. Initially I had more confidence in my degree than it deserved. I quickly learned it was difficult for a history major to qualify for any job in the business world. After several months of looking, I once again adopted my pre-college expectation of a job — anything as long as it paid.

Such was my introduction to working in the "real world." Landing a job as an administrative assistant for a small insurance association, I was relieved to be finally employed. Within weeks I was asked to write a monthly column for the association's newsletter. What luck! I had not only found a job that paid but also one with some public relations potential.

Even as I typed the boss's work, did the bookkeeping, and licked the envelopes, I wrote articles, learned new skills, and took home a paycheck that paid my expenses with a little left over for fun.

After a couple of years I began to feel the desire to look for a new challenge. With this desire also came the anxiety that gripped my heart just thinking about another job search. Fortunately, this situation coincided with a new awareness of my relationship with Jesus, so I prayed to him, "What do I do now, Lord?"

"Keep working and wait." That wasn't exactly the answer I wanted to hear. Motivated as much by procrastination as by faith, I decided to follow his directions anyway. Wasn't I surprised to see what happened!

First, I was able to arrange a month off from work to take a trip to Europe. Then my columns began to attract the attention of several influential people in the insurance industry, and I was invited to speak at a seminar. If that wasn't exciting enough, my speech was published in its entirety in the industry's major weekly newspaper. I seemed to be on a roll.

Then, without forewarning, the office was relocated twenty miles outside the city. It took me three hours to commute by bus and train to and from work each day because I didn't own a car. Add that stress to the boredom I was beginning to feel — a result of tasting the excitement of challenge and the sweetness of success — and you had a Martha determined to find a new job.

Yet I still heard the Lord say, "Wait." With three hours on a bus and train each day, our conversations were often long and heated. Rebelliously I responded, "Wait for what?"

Within a month after my speech was published, I received my answer over the phone. A convention planner asked me to speak at a major insurance company's sales conferences in Hawaii. Imagine my surprise and delight!

It meant not looking for a job for at least three months so that I could accept the invitation, but in that time God's wisdom in waiting continued to unfold. My speech was inserted into the Congressional Record, and my employer made the decision to publish my columns in a booklet entitled *My First Look At the Real World*. I thank the Lord to this day for his guidance and his grace to follow it even in the midst of stress and doubt.

When the waiting was over, I was amazed how quickly and easily things fell into place for my next job. Within a month I took a position as legislative aide in the Washington office of my hometown congressman and moved 700 miles across the country.

Working in the shadow of the U.S. Capitol was exciting. I was in charge of answering the congressman's constituent mail and handling some press relations. I learned much about America, our government, and how the democratic process works and doesn't work. After gaining valuable legislative experience through my two years "on the Hill," I decided to look for a full-fledged public relations position back in the private sector.

Due to a reorganization of the congressman's office, I did not have the option of "waiting" as I had in my first job. I suddenly found myself unemployed. If I had felt insecure and frightened looking for a job when I still lived under my parents' roof, it was nothing compared to trying to pay for the roof over my head while searching for that elusive public relations job. It had only been two years since I had been on a "high," speaking in Hawaii and autographing my booklet, so this unemployment "low" hit hard. What had happened?

I directed the question to Jesus. In the past he had answered me through the Bible, but this time he reminded me of Rudyard Kipling's poem "If" and one line in particular: "If you can meet with triumph and disaster, and treat these two imposters just the same. . . ."

It was easy to see that my triumph had been Hawaii and that my disaster was unemployment. But what was Jesus trying to tell me about "imposters"? With that question I began a prayerful reflection on my career — on where it had been and where it was going.

First, Jesus showed me how I had allowed my job to assume too much importance in my life. I had looked to my job for my identity and my fulfillment. I had let the person I worked for determine who I was and the paycheck determine how much I was worth. I had not looked within myself to find myself, and therefore my self-esteem was vulnerable to the inevitable peaks and valleys in my career. To top this off, Jesus explained that, since I judged myself on the basis of my job, I easily fell into the trap of judging others according to what they did or where they worked, and that was not his way of relating to people.

Jesus also told me I often neglected him on the job. I couldn't argue with his first revelations to me, but to this one I retorted, "But I went to Mass every time I was faced with writing a column.

I prayed before every speech and tried to squeeze your name into my text when I could."

Even as these words came forth, in my mind's eye I could see Jesus looking at me lovingly and shaking his head as he said, "But what about when you were bored? Did you offer your boredom to me in praise and thanksgiving for having a job, or did you only ask to be relieved of it? You spoke my name from the podium, and that was good. But it is better to give witness to me in action by doing your job diligently, cheerfully, and with thoughtful concern for others. And how often did you question my timing? Do you really trust me with your career?"

I heard the truth Jesus spoke to me. I prayed for the grace to make it part of my being and part of my next job, whatever it was to be and whenever it was to come.

In Jesus' timing I was offered an executive public relations position with a major insurance agents' association. At long last I was officially employed in public relations. The position offered opportunities to use my God-given talents of writing and speaking, so I picked up the pen and stood at the podium for my new employer.

This time, however, I applied the lessons I had learned from Jesus. I took *everything* to Jesus in prayer — not just the articles and speeches but also the letters and memos, my relationships with colleagues and secretaries, and the decisions I made. I put little reminders of Jesus on my desk lest I forget my good intentions.

I had previously attended daily Mass in times of stress or when I had an article to write. Then I began to go as often as possible. My prayer intentions expanded too. I continued to ask Jesus to help me write and speak well. More importantly, I prayed to be cheerful, cooperative, and tolerant on the job. I prayed about my relationships with others and saw my prayers answered.

Again, in Jesus' perfect timing, I have been promoted; my salary has increased, and my speaking has taken me on the road and on TV. I have been given the opportunity to enhance my talents by learning new skills. I have been blessed with a pleasant work environment and good people for whom and with whom to work.

By thanking Jesus for my job and its many benefits and opportunities, and by daily asking Jesus to be present with me on the job, I have also learned to keep my job and career in perspective. I give my best and earn my just wage, but I no longer expect the job to create my self-image and provide my life's satisfaction.

On the job, through the job, with a job and without one, Jesus has taught me. I have learned to wait, to praise him in the midst of boredom or tension, to trust him when unemployed, to acknowledge him in the big and little moments, to seek him first and always for my sense of fulfillment and self-worth. Indeed, I have given him my career. Looking back, I realize I could never have planned the progression I have already experienced.

I shall continue to seek Jesus' vision and timing in my career, even as I strive to follow Saint Paul's advice in every job I work: "Whatever you do, whether in speech or in action, do it in the name of the Lord Jesus. Give thanks to God the Father through him" (Colossians 3:17).

16

Spending
God's Money

Dinner was done, but no one left the table. We were deep in discussion. I was sharing my financial worries with my sister and brother-in-law who were listening intently.

I had just made a major move from Chicago to the Washington, DC, area at my expense. My cost of living had doubled with no roommate to split the rent, and my salary remained the same. I was feeling more than pinched.

In the eyes of my listeners I saw understanding and empathy. Imagine my surprise when they said to me, "Martha, do you tithe?" My immediate response was, "Do I what?" And so began the discussion that was to dramatically change my attitude about money and how I spent it.

Opening the Bible, they suggested I read Deuteronomy 14:22: "Each year you shall tithe all the produce that grows in the field you have sown." I read, but I still didn't understand what these instruments of the Lord were trying to explain to me. They directed me to read several more passages.

"Honor the LORD with your wealth,
    with first fruits of all your produce;
Then will your barns be filled with grain,
    with new wine your vats will overflow."
(Proverbs 3:9-10)

"In generous spirit pay homage to the LORD,
    be not sparing of freewill gifts.
With each contribution show a cheerful countenance
    and pay your tithes in a spirit of joy.

Give to the Most High as he has given to you,
  generously, according to your means."
(Sirach 35:7-9)

"He who sows sparingly, will reap sparingly, and he who sows bountifully will reap bountifully. Everyone must give according to what he has inwardly decided; not sadly, not grudgingly, for God loves a cheerful giver. God can multiply his favors among you so that you may always have enough of everything and even a surplus for good works." (2 Corinthians 9:6-8)

Our discussion continued. Before the end of the evening, they had shared with me their own personal experience with giving ten percent of their income to the Church or charity. They also told me of the many blessings they had received since they had begun this practice, not the least being a peace of mind about their finances.

I listened, but I still wasn't completely convinced. Having just told them how I was having trouble making ends meet, they continued to tell me to give ten percent of my income to charity. They quickly added that ten percent of my net income would be fine. I chuckled.

But the seed had been planted. Payday came, and I found myself staring at my checkbook wondering, "Should I or shouldn't I?" Coward that I was, I decided to deduct the ten percent in my check register but refrain from writing any checks against this amount until I was sure I could make it to the next payday. Surprisingly, I made it.

The sum of money involved nearly equaled my entire charitable contribution of the year preceding, and I suddenly felt embarrassed and repentant. "Oh Lord, how could I have been so stingy in the past?" But my spirits lifted when I realized I now had the pleasure of deciding who would be the recipients of my tithe.

My parish was first on my list. Then I decided to adopt a child through the Christian Children's Fund. And I still had more to give. Remembering a home for the handicapped, built and funded by a group of fellow parishioners back in Chicago, I decided to become a monthly contributor.

What a feeling of satisfaction and peace filled my heart as I wrote those checks. When payday came again, the burdensome chore of paying bills became a task I anticipated as I pondered who would be the recipient of this paycheck's tithe.

Blessings came my way. My finances seemed to take care of themselves. I specifically recall one incident when I had run short but had promised to visit a friend in Boston who needed consolation because of a broken engagement. I committed myself to going and, then, searched for an airfare that I hoped I could afford. Usually shunning the charge card when I don't have the money to back it up, I charged the flight anyway. That night I found a check in the mailbox for $77.00 — the exact amount I needed. It was my state income tax refund, but it was the timing that left me awed.

Speaking of income tax, that was another advantage I discovered about tithing. I accumulated enough charitable deductions to itemize my income taxes and pay less, despite the fact that I was single and a renter without the natural deductions of dependents and mortgage interest.

Tithing was only the beginning of my ever-expanding awareness of what it means to be a steward of God's money. After two years of tithing without question or doubt, I was faced with a test — unemployment. I was eligible for unemployment compensation, but if I thought I had been pinched before, it was nothing compared to this. Surely God wouldn't expect me to tithe my unemployment check. Or would he?

I really wrestled with this question. My answer came when week after week the bureaucracy could not explain why my first check had not arrived. For ten weeks I was forced to live off my meager, but previously sacred savings. By the time my check arrived there was no longer any question in my mind whose money it was. It was God's, and to him I would give the first fruits — my tithe.

Amazingly, even before I landed a full-time job again, I replaced the funds I had taken from my savings. Not only had God solidified the lesson of tithing in my heart and mind but also I had learned how frugally I could live.

My awareness of how to spend God's money continues to deepen. Paying a mortgage on a single person's salary has made my finances once again very tight, but since I began to think of my money as God's money, my attitude about possessions has changed.

I hear the wisdom proclaimed in the Letter to the Hebrews: "Do not love money but be content with what you have, for God has said, 'I will never desert you, nor will I forsake you' " (Hebrews 13:5).

As a result of regular prayer and meditation on the value of my earthly possessions, I am learning to resist the media hype and peer pressure that would make me think I need more than I have, or that I want more than I need. God has instilled in me a growing satisfaction with what I have and a peace about what I don't have.

I have learned that possessions have a way of possessing us. They cry out to be used and maintained. They restrict our physical mobility and our spiritual ability to submit everything to the will of God. They can lull us into a false comfort and security, and turn our attention away from our everlasting security in Jesus Christ.

When I was faced with the prospect of replacing my nine-year-old car, my attitude about possessions was tested. I was attracted to a model of car that many of my peers owned. It was sporty, foreign, definitely "in," and expensive. Once again I had to let go of my own desire for something and submit my will to God's.

Through the thoughtfulness of friends who remembered I was in the market for a car, a reliable, used, American corporation-fleet compact car was made available to me at half the market price. Thanks to a temporary loan from my parents and my subsequent tax-refund check to pay off this loan, I was able to purchase the car with cash.

Hoping to reduce the pressure on my finances, I tried to sell my old car. Even as I made this effort, something gnawed at me. Could God be suggesting I donate it? I finally found a buyer, but the nagging in my soul wouldn't go away. I decided to investigate donating my old car to charity.

One call put me in touch with a gentleman operating an organization that supplies cars to poor people. The name of his organization is "II-C-8." It stands for 2 Corinthians, chapter 8. He explained the procedure, and I responded that I had to think about it. When I hung up the phone I turned to 2 Corinthians 8.

I read the entire chapter, but meditated on this passage: "Carry it through now to a successful completion, so that your ready resolve may be matched by giving according to your means. The willingness to give should accord with one's means, not go beyond them. The relief of others ought not to impoverish you: there should be a certain equality. Your plenty at the present time should supply their need so that their surplus may one day supply your need, with equality as a result. It is written, 'He who gathered much had no excess and he who gathered little had no lack' '' (2 Corinthians 8:11-15).

I prayed. While I yearned for the additional cash in my pocket, I couldn't stop meditating on this passage. Finally, remembering that the car I was selling had been given to me and that the car I was buying was practically a gift, I decided to give my old car to someone who really needed it.

I feel good for having listened to Jesus' gentle promptings and for having shared my wealth with another. Moreover, I will be able to take the donation as a charitable deduction on my income tax. Things do have a way of being "equal" when we submit our will to God's.

What began five years ago with a simple after-dinner question — "Do you tithe?" — has developed into a tried and proven method for spending God's money.

17

My Little Bit of Heaven

My little bit of heaven is my home.

When I was a child, my home consisted of a mother and father, seven kids, and one dog in a big house. Even when I was a young adult living on my own, I still called 1501 Hillridge "home."

Things began to change when the younger kids left home and my parents relocated to a lakefront condominium. One year on my own became two, three, four. Before I knew it, I could count eight years of living "away from home." Over the course of these changes, I noticed my understanding of "home" changing too.

When I first moved away, I settled into a small studio apartment. Having shared a bedroom all my life, I appreciated having a room to myself, despite the fact it was all I had.

I was there only a year when I decided to move into a large two-bedroom apartment with a roommate. I not only had a bedroom to myself, I also had a sun-room off the living room and a full-sized refrigerator in the kitchen. It felt more permanent than my previous abode.

The living room may have been furnished in the style I have heard many singles call "early attic" and my couch may have been a single bed with bolster pillows, but apartment life was beginning to bring some sense of stability to my mind. Nonetheless, I caught the train home for every holiday because "home" was still where my parents lived.

Then I moved again, this time to a new city and to a one-bedroom apartment of my own. In the course of the move I gave away much of my "early attic" furnishings, so I started furnishing the new place in my own style. Over a couple of years I bought a Lazy-Boy recliner, a sofa bed to encourage visitors, and a wall unit for books and knickknacks.

My apartment began to take on my personality and a comfortable familiarity reminiscent of what I felt when I was "home." This homey feeling in a place other than "home" was new to me. Besides that, I was now farther than a train ride from my family, and so I spent some holidays away from "home." Or was I spending them in *my* home?

It was at this point in my life that my parents made their big move. After nearly twenty-five years in the same rambling house, it was a major physical and emotional step for them to move into a three-bedroom, single-level condominium. I was unable to be with them physically, but I was quick to offer my spiritual and emotional support. Concerned as I was about my parents' adjustment, I initially failed to notice the impact their move had on me.

My suppressed feelings eventually surfaced, and I was forced to deal with my own discomfort and sadness. I missed our old house, even though I loved the view of the lake from their new place. I wished for the room to spread out, even though I knew it was good that my parents no longer had to take care of a house that was much bigger than they needed. I hungered for the familiarity, the sense of belonging, and the memories evoked every time I returned to 1501 Hillridge. Home just was not the same. I began to wonder, *Is it even home for me anymore?*

I heard my answer in what I said to others: "I am going to Michigan to visit my family," instead of, "I am going home." When I slipped and said "home," I often corrected myself. Slowly and sometimes in pain, I began to adjust to the new physical and emotional reality: My parents' condominium was their home, not mine.

The pain came when I found myself asking more questions: *Then where is "home" for me? Is my meager apartment really "home" now? Can I think of my place as home when only one person lives in it and the situation seems so foreign to what I have known in the past?*

The answers to these questions did not come quickly. For a time I felt rootless, detached, lost, and confused. Letting go of the past and embracing an unknown future was unnerving and frightening.

A hard part of this thought process was the fact that I could not share it with those closest to me. How could I tell my parents that I felt homeless? They considered their home to be my home. I appreciated that, and I knew others who did not have this privilege. But I also felt God was calling me to let go. The feeling I had hurt me, and I was afraid that telling my parents about it might hurt them.

Jesus and I had many prayerful conversations on this subject. I seemed to bounce between sadness and rebellion, between missing "home" and feeling that the family made demands on me to come home. I felt like a Ping-Pong ball, bouncing between a mature acceptance of what Jesus was calling me to do and a rejection of it.

I wonder now how my family perceived what was going on in my mind. I did not mention anything to my parents, but through the grapevine I heard that my mother had commented, "Martha doesn't consider this home anymore, does she?" Just hearing this remark tugged at my heart. If only I could have explained what I was feeling. But then, I was not really sure what I was feeling and why. I knew I was not rejecting my parents or their home, but what was I doing?

Jesus knew what was happening. He and I were making my apartment into my home, and it took time. It took time to let go of the past and let new roots sink in. One day I woke up to realize I had lived in my current apartment for four years. That was a record for living in one place since I had left "home." The more I entertained people for dinner, hosted potluck parties for my parish Young Adults Group, and opened my home to out-of-town visitors, my place for one began to resemble a happy haven for many.

People seemed to feel welcomed and comfortable in *my* home. The walls seemed to absorb the love of others, and memories of precious moments lingered and warmed me after they left. Even when I was alone my place felt more and more like home.

When several members of my family spent Thanksgiving in my apartment, my heart finally acknowledged home was where I lived. Family had come to visit before, but there was something special about cooking a turkey and setting out my grandmother's silver for a holiday celebration. That gave my home its seal of approval in my heart and mind. I felt at peace and at home.

When I purchased a town house, my appreciation of home assumed new dimensions. Owning my own home gave me a sense of stability and security I had never quite felt as a renter in an apartment. The town house was more fun to decorate and furnish than the apartment had been. There was a sense of permanence in deciding matters like where to hang a picture or whether or not to hang the shutters.

My new home became my little bit of heaven. It is an end unit with windows on three sides that bring in the light and the breeze in heavenly ways. The deck out back, the garden out front, the dishwasher in the kitchen, and the little den for my desk and typewriter complete my dream house. I even love to be in it when it rains. The raindrops falling in the forested ravine nearby often lull me to sleep. My furnishings are the same as they were in my apartment, and my accents are simple: shells collected on the beach, prints collected from trips. How comfortable and familiar my little bit of heaven feels!

There was an initial period of adjustment, a time when I felt like a stranger in my town house. Now that I have lived through a full year's cycle of seasons, entertained guests on my deck, pulled out the sofa bed for visitors, and gathered memories to treasure, I can say that this little bit of heaven truly feels like home.

As cozy as Jesus has helped me to feel in my new home, he continues to remind me it is only temporary. I hear him teach me as he taught the apostles, "Do not lay up for yourselves an earthly treasure. Moths and rust corrode; thieves break in and steal. Make it your practice instead to store up heavenly treasure, which neither moths nor rust corrode nor thieves break in and steal" (Matthew 6:19-20).

My little bit of heaven is just that — "only" a little bit. Jesus is preparing for me a place far more comfortable and peaceful than anything here on earth.

"I am indeed going to prepare a place for you,
and then I shall come back to take you with me,
that where I am you also may be.
You know the way that leads where I go."
(John 14:3)

Trusting in Jesus' promise to us and striving to follow his ways, we should continue to build warm, welcoming homes, while knowing that, as Saint Paul says, " . . . when the earthly tent in which we dwell is destroyed we have a dwelling provided for us by God, a dwelling in the heavens, not made by hands but to last forever" (2 Corinthians 5:1).

As singles, it can be difficult for us to make the emotional transition from our parents' homes to our own individual homes. Let's consider it a foreshadowing of the eventual transition from our earthly life to our heavenly home with Jesus. Whether death occurs gradually or suddenly, peacefully or painfully, we know it will bring rich reward if we continue to seek Jesus and store up "heavenly treasure."

In the meantime, let's thank God for our homes and our little bits of heaven on earth.

18

My Home
for the Holidays

The song "I'll Be Home for Christmas" took on special meaning the year I moved away from home and anticipated returning for the Christmas holidays. While my circumstances and those portrayed in the song certainly differed, I identified with the longing for home, for tradition, and for family at Christmastime.

I love the anticipation and preparation for Christmas as much as the day itself. In the early years of my single life, I would take an extra day off before Christmas in order to share in the cookie-making and last-minute shopping with my family back home.

Then things began to change, and so did my attitudes about Christmas, cookies, and shopping. It has been a gradual process, combining the changing circumstances of my family with my own deepening relationship with the Jesus whose birth we celebrate on Christmas.

My sisters and brothers became spouses and parents. From year to year faces came and went at the Christmas dinner table. Equal time for in-laws was the first reason one or another could not be with us. Then, as children came on the scene, some of my siblings expressed the desire to stay in their respective homes in order to establish Christmas traditions of their own. Everyone else's life and Christmas practices seemed to be changing except mine.

Every Christmas I traveled "home." I made the traditional cookies and was present for Christmas Eve dinner, Midnight Mass and the Christmas Day gift exchange and buffet. Some of the family traditions of my youth were continued for a time, but after a while most faded. Even the stockings went unfilled one year, and I was given my empty stocking to pack in my suitcase and take back with me.

One Christmas Eve it became apparent that only my parents and I would be home for dinner. The pangs of change stabbed my heart. I worried that my parents might be more jarred by this threesome than I was. I quickly made arrangements to bring the dinner, plus my parents, to my brother's place; he and my sister-in-law had to stay home with their child who was sick. We had a lovely time at my brother's, but the arrangement reminded us all too vividly that things were different.

That happened a few years ago. Since then, every year when the holidays roll around I find myself questioning what I do and why I do what I do to celebrate Christmas. Last year I detected a resentment and emptiness that I hadn't realized was within me. Discovering this, I decided it was time to address the issue seriously and prayerfully.

I turned to Jesus with the many questions and concerns that surfaced. First on the list was: Do I really *want* to be in my own home for the holidays, or am I merely fatigued by the hassles of bad weather and big crowds when I travel over the holidays?

Is the emptiness I feel a response to the family Christmas traditions? If so, why? Does it stem from feeling left out because I am not raising a family of my own and establishing my own traditions like my siblings?

Does my wanting to stay home for Christmas flow from a selfish desire or from a desire to give selflessly? If it flows from a selfless desire, how would I express that desire differently in my home versus my parents' home?

And finally: What is it about the liturgy, the family gift-giving, and the excessive eating that leaves me feeling uncomfortable and out of place? Is it that in my parents' parish I feel like an observer, whereas in my own parish I feel like a participant? What about gift-giving and eating? Isn't that what Christmas is all about? How and why have my attitudes changed?

Such a string of questions Jesus and I are discussing. Our discussion is ongoing because I haven't found all the answers yet. I am trying to be open to Jesus' answers and to give up my own selfish desires. It is a heartrending process.

My heart rends because I feel pulled in different directions by good options. Part of me wants to be with my family in my parents' home, and part of me wants to be in my own home. Part of me yearns for the traditions of old, while part of me yearns to establish traditions of my own. I like attending Mass with my blood family, but I also cherish singing and participating in the liturgy with my faith family. I enjoy good eating and opening presents, but have I considered the ways Jesus may be asking me to share what I have with others less fortunate?

Even as I ask these questions, Jesus quickly reminds me that while some family traditions may no longer be meaningful for me, I must continue to be sensitive to the feelings of others. My family may not be feeling the need to alter Christmas practices, and they may have no idea of my feelings regarding the status quo. Somehow, with the grace of God, I shall strike a balance between being sensitive to the feelings of my family and being true to myself and to my awareness of what Jesus may be calling me to do.

When I shared with some single friends my feelings and questions — and, specifically, my desire to be in my own home for the holidays — I found I was not alone in this struggle. In discussions with other Christian singles, I have learned how they have answered some of the questions I am pondering.

One single male friend is a regular visitor to an orphanage in town. On Christmas Day he brings five or six of the children to his family's Christmas gathering. His family has chosen not to exchange gifts. Instead, they pool their money and throw a party for friends and neighbors and whomever else they can entice to come eat, sing Christmas carols, and pray together.

Another friend could not travel to her family's midwestern home for Christmas one year because of financial constraints. She took the opportunity to celebrate Christmas her way. She attended her community's liturgy, served breakfast to homeless women in a shelter where she regularly volunteers, and cooked dinner for friends who, like herself, were far from family on Christmas Day.

The loving, selfless examples of these two friends spur me on to keep seeking Jesus' answers to my questions about how I am to celebrate the birth of our loving, giving Redeemer.

Already I am considering alternatives for next Christmas. The word is out that all siblings, spouses, and children will be gathering at my parents' on Christmas Day this year for the first time in four or five years. This is definitely not the year to choose to be absent.

In the meantime, I am considering singing with my folk group at Midnight Mass on Christmas Eve and flying home on Christmas Day. This arrangement could give me a little of both worlds. I could be home, in my home, for the anticipation of Christmas. I could participate in my faith community's liturgy and avoid the pre-Christmas holiday rush at the airport. And I could still be in Michigan in time for Christmas dinner and the gift exchange with the family, hopefully with a heart open and sensitive to their feelings and preferences.

While I won't be able to host orphans for Christmas dinner or serve breakfast to homeless women, I do have an ideal opportunity to reach out to the less fortunate. While visiting my eighty-three-year-old disabled grandmother in a nursing home, I could spread a little cheer with cookies and song among her resident neighbors, especially among those who won't have any visitors. In this small way I could share my blessings with those in need.

These ideas are just *maybes* because Jesus and I are still discussing my options. I realize I am blessed with a family and with health and finances which give me the opportunity to make a choice. For other singles, especially those without family or those with dependent children, options are more limited. Recognizing this painful reality, I am reminded to pray for my single peers, especially at Christmastime.

As for my choice, I have made no holiday travel plans yet. I am seeking Jesus' will in the decisions I make about Christmas, trusting that these decisions will be sensitive to the feelings of others and true to myself and to him.

It is sometimes difficult for singles to acknowledge the desire to celebrate Christmas in their own homes, in their own way. It is even harder for others, especially parents, to understand it. As we search our own hearts and seek God's will in our Christmas celebrations, let's remember the words the angel spoke to the shepherds on that first Christmas night: ''You have nothing to fear! I come to proclaim good news to you — tidings of great joy to be shared by the whole people. This day in David's city a savior has been born to you, the Messiah and Lord'' (Luke 2:10-11).

Jesus is Lord. When we ask, he will tell us how he wants us to celebrate his birthday with him and his people.

19

The Joys
of Travel

It was only a quick jaunt between Nashville and Washington, but when the plane lifted off the ground, so did my spirits. The farther we moved from the earth, the more relaxed I became. I leaned back in my seat to bask once again in the freedom I feel when I am flying.

It really matters not whether I am taking off in an airplane on a short flight or merging on the expressway at the beginning of a cross-country trek, or whether I am traveling for business or pleasure — I feel a surge of excitement every time I begin a trip. I love to travel.

I love meeting new people, seeing new places, tasting different food. I love that feeling of leaving responsibilities behind me and entering a world of new experiences. I delight in anticipating and wondering what surprises a trip might hold for me.

I enjoy traveling to places where family and friends live. I like to visit their homes, play with their children, meet their friends. My relationships with them deepen as I mix and mingle with people on their turf, as I eat at their table, as I see where they work and how they live.

Traveling is one of the benefits of single life that I most enjoy and probably capitalize on most often. My single, no-strings-attached lifestyle gives me the freedom to choose how I spend my time and money. When it comes to time off from work, my first thought is: Where do I want to go? When it comes to business travel, I quickly review my address book to see what family and friends live near where I must travel. When it comes to spending money, I wonder what I can do without in order to save for my next trip.

I have definitely capitalized on this freedom to travel, having visited forty-seven of our United States, Canada, Mexico, eight countries in Europe, and two in the Mideast. As I crossed the Suez Canal on a ferry, I had the thrill of hearing the tour guide say I was leaving the continent of Asia and entering the continent of Africa.

I know many singles enjoy staying closer to home and renting a cottage at the beach or on a nearby lake for a week or two. Summertime visits with my parents at the lake and long weekends with friends at the beach are my choice, too, when the vacation is a short one. When it comes to long vacations, however, I am a free spirit who prefers to board a plane and fly off to distant lands.

As singles, many of us have the freedom to choose where we go, how long we stay, and what we do. We do not have to be concerned about a spouse's preference, the children's needs, or a religious community's money restrictions. We are the decision-makers, and when it comes to travel it is wonderful to be single.

Certainly, there are some drawbacks for singles traveling. Finding a ride to and from the airport is one example. It is an expensive endeavor if a taxi is the only choice, or an extra effort to find a friend to provide the ride. While trips abroad are fun-filled, they are better shared with someone special. Sometimes it is hard to find someone who can go where I want to go, for the same number of days off work, and at the time of year I can go. Often we singles have to take a tour or go alone and deal with the periodic loneliness that comes with having no one with whom to share the experiences.

Through these challenges of single travel I have learned the value of seeking God's guidance in making my choices and the value of trusting him to fulfill my needs and desires. We are quick to seek this guidance in times of trouble, but I believe God wants to be intimately included in our fun times too. Often he enhances these fun times in ways we could never imagine. Here are a couple of examples of what I mean.

Two years into my career I arranged a month's leave of absence to travel to Europe. It was a trip I had dreamed about since high school, and I finally saw the possibility of making this dream come true. But — I was faced with traveling alone. I asked God over and over again whether it was really the time to make this trip. I was uneasy about traveling alone, yet somehow at peace with the timing of the trip. So I proceeded with my plans.

Six weeks before I was to take off, I flippantly asked my nineteen-year-old brother if he wanted to waltz through Europe with me. Needing a break from college, he decided a European trip with big sister would be great. With some help from Mom and Dad, my brother accompanied me.

We never did waltz, but we regaled in Munich's Oktoberfest, inhaled Switzerland's mountainous beauty, paled before the Louvre's magnificent masterpieces, and Eurailed through flower-studded towns and velvet valleys. We enjoyed all that we saw and did on this once-in-a-lifetime trip, and it was made extra-special because we shared it as brother and sister.

Our lives have gone in divergent directions since that trip, but my brother and I both feel a unique bond that can never be broken because of our shared European experience. Little could I have known what God had in store for my brother and me. How thankful I am. How glad I am that I asked God for his input.

Last year I had the opportunity to take another trip abroad. This time I was sitting at Mass when the priest announced he was escorting a pilgrimage to the Holy Land. The family members who were with me at the Mass expressed interest, and their interest piqued mine even though I shy away from large group tours.

As it turned out, everyone else in the family decided they couldn't go on the pilgrimage. I found myself faced with the prospect of taking a trip with a large group of people I didn't know. What's more, it meant postponing a trip to Ireland I had been planning. After asking for God's guidance, I decided to make the pilgrimage.

For reasons I will never know, the tour consisted of only six people, including the priest. What a break for this free spirit! Plus, God gave me not one but two special people with whom to share the trip intimately.

Four of us were in our twenties and thirties. But it was a widow in her fifties, a mother of seven children, who became my special friend. We shared the depth of feeling evoked while visiting the holy places of Jesus, but we also enjoyed the fun of lunch at a sidewalk cafe in Rome and the laughter that comes when you trip over each other as roommates for two weeks.

The priest also became very special to me. God blessed our group with a man who obviously knew Jesus and the Word of God in an intimate and prayerful way. Our experience of the Holy Land was enhanced by his knowledge and his piety. This humble man of God made our Masses in Bethlehem, in Cana, in a chapel on the Via Dolorosa, and in the privacy of a hotel room times of deep sharing with our Lord. Besides that, the priest was lots of fun, too.

God has always revealed much to me about himself and his Church through my travels. When I was a child and our family traveled, my parents sought out the spiritual sites in places we visited — places such as Sainte Anne de Beaupré in Quebec, the Shrine of the Immaculate Conception and the Franciscan Monastery in Washington, DC, and the mission churches in California. I continue this practice in my single travels, and my relationship with Jesus has continued to grow because of it.

In Germany, thanks to my Jesuit friend living in Munich, my brother and I learned about the theology behind the architecture we saw in the cathedrals. In England, like Chaucer's pilgrims, we visited Canterbury to pay our respect to the memory of Saint Thomas à Becket. My decision to take the trip to the Holy Land was based on the hope that my understanding of Jesus, his Mother, his ancestors, and his apostles would deepen. An added benefit to the pilgrimage was a visit to Assisi and Rome, where the lives of Saint Francis and Saint Peter especially touched me.

God has blessed my travels with safety, with magnificent views, new taste treats, and new friends. He has opened my eyes, ears, and heart to a world beyond my own. I have seen the many, many differences in people, culture, language, and attitude, and I have grown more open, tolerant, and appreciative of these differences. And through it all, I have been given a deeper awareness and appreciation of the magnificent Creator who made our world with all its differences and delights.

While my eyes have seen the wonder, they have also seen the pain and evil. Brushing shoulders with a soldier's machine gun in Jerusalem, passing the beggars in most major cities I have visited here and abroad, seeing the discrimination and repression of freedom — these memories remind me that opened eyes demand

active hands. Jesus continually calls me to see him in everyone —
rich and poor, friend and enemy, accepted and rejected — and to
extend my hands in justice, compassion, and peace as he would.

Travel offers much to single Christians in terms of fun and
excitement, but it can also have a significant impact on our
relationship with Jesus. By seeking his will in the travel choices we
make, we invite him to travel with us. In addition to the slides and
souvenirs we bring home to share with others, may we also bring
home a renewed spirit of acceptance and generosity toward all of
God's people.

Lord, where shall we go next?

20

In Times
of Struggle

She had lost thirty pounds and two inches, but her brown eyes sparkled with the joy that was always her own. Struggling to stand up, she turned to ask me, in her distinctive Dutch accent, "Would you like some more, Honey?" I jumped to my feet to assist her, but she insisted that I remain seated so that she could serve me.

My widowed friend was battling cancer for the second time in two years. With a peace and joy that left me in awe, she was enduring chemotherapy and the side effects of pain medication. She told me about her long nights sleeping in a chair because to sleep in her bed was to risk being unable to get out of bed in the morning. She shared with me her pain, her loneliness, her confusion, but also her faith.

She asked questions about my job and my friends, told me about hers, and insisted on paying for lunch when we were together. We laughed, we cried, and we prayed. Each time I left her, I reflected on how faithful, how patient, how selfless she was in the midst of such agony.

I have another friend who is enduring a struggle of a different kind. Eight months pregnant with her second child and with a 16-month-old to care for, she was abandoned by her husband for another woman. Such shock, such rejection, such reason for depression and despair. But not for this friend. Armed with a faith in Christ that directed her to spend more time praying and reading the Scriptures, she bounced back. She resolved to spend more quiet time with the Lord, even as she chased her energetic toddler by day and fed her newborn by night.

Struggling to raise her children and maintain her sense of self-worth, she has little time to associate with people outside her immediate family. For two years my only contact with her has been by phone and on an annual Christmas visit. Every time we talk she proclaims God's faithfulness to her and her children, even as she shares with me her down times and her agonizing nights with a daughter who can't sleep because Daddy doesn't live with them anymore.

Despite her personal pain, she also remains interested in what is happening in my life. Believe it or not, she even asks about the men I am dating. What a faithful, selfless person she is in the midst of such a struggle.

"Accept whatever befalls you,
  in crushing misfortune be patient.
For in fire gold is tested,
  and worthy men in the crucible of humiliation.
Trust God and he will help you;
  make straight your ways and hope in him."
(Sirach 2:4-6)

Thinking about my two friends, this Scripture passage has new meaning. They are patient in the face of misfortune. They trust God when things happen that they don't understand. His love and peace are shining clearly through their lives.

We all have our own struggles in life. Some may be as heart-rending as sickness and separation, disability or the death of a loved one. Other struggles may appear on the surface to be less intense, but they are still very real: an unfulfilling job, months of unemployment, broken romances or friendships, strained relationships with parents or siblings, constant battles with finances. The list is as long and diverse as the people caught in the varied situations of life.

In times of struggle, singles often have the additional challenge of enduring them alone. A single person described this challenge in one sentence of a letter she wrote to me, "When my Dad died, my sisters leaned on their husbands, I leaned on me, and we all leaned on God."

I can relate to her comment because when my grandmother died, I had a similar experience. The night before she died, the doctors were unsure of her status, so I immediately caught a train home to be with her and my family. Her parting words, "See you in the morning, darling," were never to come true. In the morning, I stood with my mother by my grandmother's bedside and watched her die.

For the next four days my family was together constantly as we went through the wake and funeral. When it was all over, I boarded the train to return alone to my apartment in the big city. I felt lonelier than I can ever remember. The grief of losing a grandmother who had been such a big part of my life was only beginning to sink in, and I had to deal with it miles from anyone who could really share it with me. It was a very real sorrow and struggle for me.

Alone as we may be in the physical world, it is important for single Christians to remember, especially in times of struggle, that Jesus is with us. We are not climbing our personal Calvary alone. Jesus is walking each step of the way with us. As we endure the Good Fridays in our lives, we must not forget the victory of Easter Sunday that Jesus gave us.

One way for me to remember this spiritual reality is to meditate on Saint Paul's words to the Romans in chapter eight. While the whole chapter sheds insight on the meaning of suffering in our lives, I am especially touched by these words: "But if we are children, we are heirs as well: heirs of God, heirs with Christ, if only we suffer with him so as to be glorified with him. I consider the sufferings of the present to be as nothing compared with the glory to be revealed in us" (Romans 8:17-18).

We believe in Christ's Resurrection. We know the victory of Easter is ours. In times of struggle we must claim the victory. We must banish the devils of doubt and despair, of fear and anxiety. We must heed the advice given in the letter to the Thessalonians, "Rejoice always, never cease praying, render constant thanks; such is God's will for you in Christ Jesus" (1 Thessalonians 5:16-18).

Suffering is inevitable in this life. We will have our crosses to bear; but if we trust in God's power and give thanks always, God will empower us with the strength not only to endure our sufferings but also to give witness to his saving presence in our lives. In times of struggle, we have the opportunity to show others the glory and victory that is ours through Christ, in this life as well as in eternity.

This truth was imbedded in my heart when I experienced the emotional and financial struggle of unemployment. Remembering Saint Paul's words to give thanks in all situations, I turned to Jesus in prayer and in gratitude. He in turn gave me his peace and a deeper appreciation of how he suffered for me.

Jesus reassured me that he was with me by once again bringing to my mind the image of the two of us walking hand in hand. This time I became aware of the hole in his hand. My heart stopped. He invited me, as he once invited the apostle Thomas, to probe the holes in his hands and to meditate on his Passion and death. As I did, I was humbled by how Jesus endured suffering. In the midst of the worst kind of struggle, humiliation, and pain, Jesus trusted his Father's will and continued to show his love and concern for others.

In the garden he reached out to heal the man whose ear had been cut off. Before Pilate he held his tongue when he could have justified himself. On the Cross he forgave the thief and lovingly entrusted his Mother to the beloved disciple. In the end he forgave those who crucified him and willingly surrendered his spirit to his Father.

As Christians, we are called to follow Jesus to Calvary, to walk in his footsteps, to probe the holes in his hands, and to accept when our own are pierced. God does not *inflict* suffering on those he loves, but *allows* it, as he allowed it in the life of his only Son. Suffering enables us to grow closer to God and come to know the victory that is ours through Jesus. If we follow Jesus' example of trusting the Father and reaching out to others in the midst of our own suffering, his victory will be our victory.

We cannot remove the crosses from our lives. We cannot control all circumstances, but we can control our response to them. We can claim Jesus' victory and grow through the struggle, or we can turn away, waver in our faith, and allow the struggle to consume us. God has given us the power to endure suffering and even conquer it through the risen Jesus. It is up to us to believe and to ask God to pour forth the Holy Spirit upon us.

I have seen one friend face cancer and another suffer rejection and abandonment. In their pain they have demonstrated a peace and selfless concern for others that could only come from God through their faith in the victory of his Son. As we face the struggles of our lives now and in the future, may the witness of these two women inspire us. Like them may we find strength, courage, and comfort promised by the prophet Isaiah:

"They that hope in the LORD will renew their strength,
   they will soar as with eagles' wings;
They will run and not grow weary,
   walk and not grow faint."
(Isaiah 40:31)

21

Discovering the Meaning of Friendship

Climbing up and down three flights of stairs, carrying everything from boxes of books to mattresses, my friends helped me move so I wouldn't have to hire an expensive mover.

Lending me their car to drive twenty miles to and from work, five days a week for nearly nine months, my friends came to my rescue when I needed time to look for a new job that was accessible by bus.

My friends have picked me up at the airport when I needed a ride home. They have picked me up emotionally with a phone call, a card, or a trip to the ice cream shop when my spirits needed a lift.

My friends also include my sisters and brothers and their spouses. They have generously given me their hand-me-downs, including a stereo and a microwave, and have paid the shipping costs besides.

Just the other day, a friend spent three hours, on her day off, in the doctor's office with me. I could have driven myself, but she knew, without my asking, that her companionship would comfort me.

When I think of the word "friend," I immediately think of the woman to whom this book is dedicated. We met when I was fourteen. Our friendship has grown despite the fifteen years difference in age and the hundreds of miles now separating us. This book is dedicated to her because she affirmed the creativity she saw in me before I saw it in myself. With the gift of a book entitled *Maybe You Should Write a Book,* she planted the seed that now bears fruit on these pages. This book's dedication is a mere token of my affection and appreciation.

When I think of friends I think of many people who have loved me, shared their lives with me, helped me, and challenged me to be all that I can be. I think of my Alpha Delta Pi sorority sisters and the members of the Young Adult Group from my Chicago neighborhood parish. I think of the people I have met at a parish renewal, through Cursillo, in the choir, and on the job. I think of people twenty-five and forty-five years my senior and fifteen years my junior. I think of married couples with families of several children, and I think of single parents and people with elderly parents who are dependent on them. And I feel especially blessed to count my sisters among my dearest friends.

Over the years I have discovered the meaning of friendship by observing what others have done for me in the name of friendship. As I have moved from one phase of life to another, from one part of the country to another, the meaning of friendship has unfolded.

From my friends I have learned that to have a friend is to be a friend. The love and generosity of my friends have called forth love and generosity from me. I am now quick to lend a helping hand to someone who is moving, to lend my car to someone without one, to write a check for someone in need, to make a call or drop a card in the mail to someone who is lonely or struggling.

I have learned that without friendship, single life would be a lonely, difficult existence. Without friendship, Christian community would mean nothing. Without friendship, Jesus would be a distant God.

Through my friends I have discovered the meaning of friendship not only in human terms but also in divine terms. Through the love of friends, I have experienced the love of Jesus and the support of Christian community.

As I have taken the risk to reveal myself to my friends, I have learned to open my heart to Jesus. As friends have loved me with all my idiosyncrasies, I have experienced Jesus loving me with all my sins. As friends have given themselves to me in time and effort, I have learned how to give myself to Jesus in prayer and loving action toward others. As I have swallowed my pride and expressed my need for help to my friends, I have learned how to confess my pride to Jesus and admit my dependence on him.

Through my friends I have experienced God's friendship. Through God's friendship I have learned how to be a better friend. The circle of God's love goes round and round, as does the ongoing discovery of the meaning of friendship.

Friendship means being present to another even when it is inconvenient or uncomfortable. It means listening without judgment or criticism and offering advice only when asked. It means feeling close and desiring to grow closer, while always acknowledging and respecting the mystery of each individual heart and soul that can never be fully understood by another.

Friendship means saying, "I love you," in word and deed, and saying it often. It is loving unconditionally. Sometimes that means letting go — albeit reluctantly — when someone chooses to end a friendship.

These are just a few of the characteristics I have discovered and tried to nurture in my friendships. The process of developing friendships is both endless and demanding, especially if we take to heart what Jesus tells us about the true test of friendship:

"There is no greater love than this:
to lay down one's life for one's friends."
(John 15:13)

Jesus calls us friends. He calls us continually to grow in our understanding of his friendship so that we may grow in our friendship with others. He calls us to follow his example and die to self that we might know the depth of the love of him who died for us. He calls us to love as he loves, so that others will come to know him as a friend.

The Cursillo movement capsulizes this call in its motto, "Make a friend, be a friend, bring a friend to Christ."

Lately, making a friend has consisted of going out to lunch with a colleague from work and playing tennis with a neighbor. Being a friend has meant brainstorming career options with my colleague and consoling my neighbor who is working through a broken romance. Bringing these new friends to Christ has included praying for them and sharing my faith with them. Bringing a friend to Christ means loving people where they are at, and also taking the risk to share with them the source of our love in the name of Jesus Christ.

A very special friend comes to mind when I think of the Cursillo motto. Neither of us can quite remember what sparked between us one day in the hall at work. We are an unlikely pair, dramatically different in age, marital status, and personality.

Our friendship grew over a period of months as we ran into each other in the hall, went for lunch, then to movies, and in time met each other's families. Gradually, we began to share more about ourselves, and our friendship deepened.

I sponsored this friend on a Cursillo weekend. Moved by her experience, she in turn sponsored a friend who traveled over 700 miles to participate in a Cursillo with her.

I befriended her disabled mother, and together we arranged for her mother to attend a retreat for the seriously ill. Since that retreat I rarely visit her mother without taking some time to pray with her.

This friend and I have grown closer through our shared journey with Jesus. We have prayed together for our families, our colleagues at work, and our world. We have seen the positive results of our prayer.

Most recently, she stood by me patiently and lovingly, shrugging off the emotional outbursts of a struggling author who periodically misdirected her frustration at her devoted friend. She showed me what sharing Christ really means. It means being Christ to others.

So what is the meaning of friendship? Jesus says it best:

"Love one another
as I have loved you."
(John 15:12)

22

The Experience of Intimacy

Intimacy. Just by saying the word, I taste, hear, and feel its meaning.

Intimacy is that precious, indescribable feeling of closeness, of tenderness, of depth, and of oneness. It is a feeling charged with energy and emotion. It bonds God to people and people to each other. Born out of love and trust, it adds richness and poignancy to our lives.

In today's society, unfortunately, much of the emotional and spiritual beauty and mystery of intimacy is overlooked or missed because of the current preoccupation with the sexual expression of intimacy. The consequence of this narrow focus has been the unspoken assumption that intimacy is only for the young, the attractive, the healthy, and the sexually active. Where does that leave the old, the sick, the disabled, the unattractive, and those who choose to live chaste lives? Are they denied the experience of intimacy? Single Christians are left wondering, "How can I experience intimacy?"

The closer Jesus has drawn me to himself, the wider he has opened my eyes to see the infinite opportunities for intimacy that he gives me because he loves me and because I respond to his love.

"Eye has not seen, ear has not heard,
    nor has it so much as dawned on man
    what God has prepared for those who love him."
(1 Corinthians 2:9)

My first conscious awareness of feeling intimate with God was awakened by the melody, harmony, and lyrics of three songs:

"Only in God" and "I Lift Up My Soul," by the St. Louis Jesuits, and "You Are Near," by the Word of God singers. In the solitude of my apartment I listened to these songs over and over again because the music lifted me up to God and gave me a sense of oneness with him.

Eventually, I realized the songs were Psalms set to music. Turning to the Scriptures I prayed these songs of old, and they spoke to me of the constancy of God's love and forgiveness and his intimate relationship with me.

"O LORD, you have probed me and you know me;
   you know when I sit and when I stand;
   you understand my thoughts from afar.
My journeys and my rest you scrutinize,
   with all my ways you are familiar."
(Psalm 139:1-3)

My experience of intimacy with God has expanded and now includes the sacraments and nature. Partaking in the Eucharist I feel Jesus' intimate touch as I become one with his body through the Bread of Life. I feel healed when, through the hands of another praying over me, I receive the Holy Spirit's gifts of peace and forgiveness. I am awestruck watching the crashing waves and the setting sun, knowing that the same God who created these wonders intimately resides in me.

"God is love,
and he who abides in love
abides in God,
and God in him."
(1 John 4:16)

Through the experience of divine intimacy, Jesus has drawn me out of myself and opened my heart to experience emotional and spiritual intimacy with others. In the daily happenings and dramatic events of life, Jesus has invited me to experience intimacy in many different ways.

Gently, I have been awakened by my toddling nephew, carrying a stuffed animal and crawling into bed with me whispering, "Aunt Martha, you need a bunny to wake you up."

Spontaneously and tenderly, intimacy grew as I was hugged by my youngest sister, and her lighthearted ways have always refreshed me.

I have been moved to tears reading letters from family and friends. My father's love has intimately touched me when I read his scribbled handwriting on a postcard "I am proud of your professional accomplishments and spiritual growth."

I have felt needed and affirmed when a friend greeted me by saying, "When I first caught a glimpse of you walking out of the airport with your luggage my heart leapt because you were home. I have missed you so."

Tears of joy have streamed down my face while praying for others. Sitting on the bed with her daughter playing at our feet, my oldest sister shared with me her deeply felt joys and fears about being a mother. Recognizing the gift of intimacy Jesus was giving us in that moment, I suggested we pray that Jesus hold her anxious heart. Our prayer ended in a hug of intimacy I shall never forget.

I have also tasted intimacy in community. On a Cursillo retreat I have shared the joy and pain of people discovering Jesus' intimate presence within themselves. During Mass I have been filled with a sense of intimacy and unity as hundreds of people joined hands and prayed the Lord's Prayer together. I have been amazed by the power and mystery of faith and prayer which draws a diverse people together.

I have experienced the intimacy of compassion without judgment as I have divulged my sins, my weaknesses, and my darker side to my spiritual director and closest friends. I have experienced the intimacy of forgiving and being forgiven as the spirit of reconciliation surged through a friendship that had been riddled with jealousy and misunderstanding. I have experienced the intimacy of glee and jubilation at the birth of nieces and a nephew. I have felt the intimacy of sorrow in the poignant moment of standing with my mother as we watched her mother die.

Intimacy is the sharing of pain as well as joy. It is the experience that brings together the physical, emotional, and spiritual facets of our lives. It is an experience that defies any and all physical limitations we might unknowingly place on it.

This lesson was impressed on my heart and mind the weekend I flew home to see my father's mother when she suffered what we thought was a second stroke. Paralyzed on her left side by her first stroke, my grandmother has been disabled and living in a nursing home for nine years. When I walked into her room and caught a glimpse of her sunken cheeks and labored breathing, I choked back my tears.

I had flown home to see her one last time, to say my good-byes, to pray with her before she died. Over the next few days I experienced many moments of intimacy with her. With my fingers I played with hers, and she cracked a smile. Brushing her hair and rubbing the one side of her back where she still had feeling, I saw an unmistakable look of pleasure and relief in her eyes.

With my grandmother, my brothers, and brother-in-law, we prayed the Lord's Prayer. With my father — her son — we prayed and asked her to repeat, ''Jesus, I love you, have mercy on me, forgive my sins, and take me to your Father.'' Sitting alone with her, she whispered to me, ''Let me kiss you.'' Before I left, I reminded her to tell Jesus when she saw him that I love him too. She responded, ''He already knows,'' and again I cried.

I said good-bye, but it may not have been my last, for she did not die. My heart aches just thinking of her disintegrating physical condition, and I wonder why Jesus has not taken her. Maybe he wants her to share a moment of intimacy with someone else before she dies. Maybe someone else needs to learn as I did that the experiences of intimacy are as unlimited as the God who gives them.

The experience of intimacy is a precious gift. It may be wrapped in moments of tremendous joy or deep suffering, in moments of playfulness or spiritual depth, in moments alone with God or shared with others.

As I have experienced such intimate moments, as I have felt and watched the Holy Spirit come upon me and others, I have become more open, more responsive, more expectant, and more spontaneous. I live my life waiting and looking for the next time God will offer me his gift of intimacy.

Jesus has blessed me with the desire to grow in intimacy with him and with others, despite the fear and embarrassment I sometimes feel. He has taught me to risk, to be vulnerable, to tear down the walls I have defensively built around my heart, and to invite others inside. He has asked me to let him inside, to set aside my pride and my need to be in control. He wants me to know him intimately by letting go and letting myself just be in his loving presence.

He has also shown me that the best way to share the gift of intimacy with others is to be loving, loyal, compassionate, trustworthy, accepting, and forgiving. He has encouraged me to grow in attentiveness and empathy as a listener. He has taught me much about intimacy, and he assures me I still have much to learn.

As I have become more open to intimacy, I have also become more aware of the pain of loneliness. I want intimacy often and always. When I don't experience it, I feel lonely. By showing me my unrealistic desire for constant intimacy, Jesus has called me and continues to call me into a mature relationship with him and with others. He has reminded me that intimacy is as precious as loneliness is painful, but that both are fleeting. Both intimacy and loneliness have the power to draw me closer to God.

Jesus' life gives witness to the labor pains of loneliness that give birth to the poignant moments of intimacy. This interrelationship between loneliness and intimacy was dramatically seen in the last days of Jesus' life.

When I imagine the scene of the Last Supper, I think of Leonardo da Vinci's painting that depicts the apostles gathered around Jesus and John laying across Jesus' chest. I see this as a picture of intimacy, and an intimacy later acted upon as Jesus, the Lord and Master, washed the feet of his friends.

Within hours of this intimate breaking of bread, however, Jesus agonized in the pit of loneliness and despair in the Garden of Gethsemane. He begged his friends saying, "My heart is nearly broken with sorrow. Remain here and stay awake with me" (Matthew 26:38). But they let him down. In the darkness, he was left alone and forsaken by those with whom he had just shared the experience of intimacy.

Jesus climbed Calvary and died on the Cross alone. He endured the most painful feeling of loneliness — the feeling of even being forgotten by his Father — "My God, my God, why have you forsaken me?'' (Mark 15:34) But it was out of this ultimate sacrifice of self in death that Jesus was raised to the height of intimacy and union with his Father through his Resurrection.

Our experiences of intimacy in this life are but a foreshadowing of the intimacy of everlasting life that Jesus' Resurrection promises us. May we embrace the moments of intimacy that Jesus gives us and endure the moments of loneliness as he did. Then one day may we meet our risen Lord face-to-face, as Mary did in that tender, joyous, intimate moment of recognition in the garden that first Easter morn, ''Mary! . . . *Rabbouni*'' (John 20:16).

Until that day, may we invite others to experience intimacy with us and with God by proclaiming as Mary did, ''I have seen the Lord!'' (John 20:18)

PART THREE

LOOKING
AHEAD

23

Facing
the Future

Facing the future. This short phrase has an ominous ring to it. Just posing the question, ''What about my future?'' stirs anxiety and fear in my heart.

Have you ever wished you could take a look at your future? When I was young, I would often ask God to give me just a pinhole peek at what lay ahead of me. He never did, and I am appreciative of his wisdom. Having lived through exciting times, trying times, and normal, everyday times, I am glad I didn't know what was to come. It might have spoiled the excitement. I might have been frightened by what I saw. I might have tried to pursue my will instead of God's.

Nonetheless, pondering my future stirs up anxiety. As a single person, I feel especially insecure about where my life is going. This anxiety has been expressed in different ways at different stages of my single life.

When I was in my early twenties, I was too busy living in the present to worry about my future. As I approached my thirties, I began to think more about marriage and children. From what older singles have shared with me, I understand that feelings about the future continue to change as careers peak and then decline, as friends have children and grandchildren, as retirement sets in, and, finally, as friends die and death draws near.

Listening to and observing other singles in the stages of life ahead of me, I often become concerned about my future. Rebelliously, I assert, ''I don't want to become bitter like so many people I have seen who have grown old alone!'' Another single person expressed a similar concern to me in her letter that said,

"At forty-seven, I find my life lonelier as time goes by. I have to guard against self-pity."

While I am happy as a single at thirty, I sometimes wonder how I will feel at forty, fifty, sixty, or seventy, with no children or grandchildren to fill my hours or at least my heart. Another letter writer echoed my questioning when she wrote, "Single is being scared to death . . . what if I should live to be old?"

One day when those thoughts crossed my mind, God brought me up short with the question, "What makes you think you are going to live until you are forty, fifty, sixty, or seventy?"

I really hadn't thought about it that way. God then reminded me of a single man whose life left me in awe and whose biography brought tears to my eyes when I read it as a teenager. That man was Dr. Tom Dooley. I had cried because his medical missionary work was cut short when he died of cancer at age thirty-four. Thirty-four! God's message to me came across loud and clear.

Life is a precious, fragile gift. In the blink of an eye the heartbeat can cease, the breathing can stop. Sickness or accident can strike at any moment, with or without warning. In my head I have always known this. In my soul I have believed that my life is truly in God's hands. I have thanked him for the gift of each day. I have given my life, my daily efforts to him, but maybe not as completely as I had thought.

I obviously still harbored some fear about my future. I worried and wondered too much about where I was going and what would happen next. What my head knew had obviously not been clearly translated into the language of the heart and soul. That language is called *trust*.

Trusting God and his plans for my future is an ongoing effort. I first became aware of my need to grow in this trust when the St. Louis Jesuits' song "Be Not Afraid" became popular. I seemed to hear it in every church I entered, no matter how far I traveled. The three verses took on different meanings, depending on the circumstances of my life, but the message, originally expressed by Isaiah, was always the same: "Fear not, for I have redeemed you . . . you are mine. . . . I will be with you . . . " (Isaiah 43:1-2).

To trust God with my future, to remember that he goes before me always, does indeed give me rest. It gives me the opportunity to live the present to the fullest and have the freedom to delight in the beauty of each moment and the strength to persevere in the midst of each trial. Trust allows me to watch the path immediately ahead of me lest I trip because I am straining to see what is around the bend. I am free to look down and notice the tiny flowers bordering the path I walk, even as I periodically look up to see the peak I am climbing. To trust is to know that as I climb the many mountains of my present life, God will ensure my travel to the ultimate peak of everlasting life.

To trust is to believe that God's words to Jeremiah apply to my life too: ''For I know well the plans I have in mind for you, says the LORD, plans for your welfare, not for woe! plans to give you a future full of hope. When you call me, when you go to pray to me, I will listen to you. When you look for me, you will find me. Yes, when you seek me with all your heart, you will find me with you'' (Jeremiah 29:11-14).

While trust in God gives me rest, it does not mean I am to disregard my future and live as if there were no tomorrow. A healthy awareness of what could lie before me is essential if I am to continue to live responsibly and use God's gifts wisely. It is important for me especially, as a single, to make thoughtful and prayerful decisions about where to live, what career path to take, how to prevent sickness, insure health care, and plan for retirement.

By making these decisions prayerfully, I seek God's will and put aside the worry and obsession the world often associates with these decisions. Jesus instructs us when he says, ''Stop worrying. The unbelievers of this world are always running after these things. Your Father knows that you need such things. Seek out instead his kingship over you, and the rest will follow in turn'' (Luke 12:29-31).

As believers in Jesus, we are called to seek God's will and to trust that the decisions he calls us to make and the path he beckons us to take are the best ones for us. They will be the best, not just because our needs will be met but because God's kingship will reign in our hearts.

I was recently reminded of this message as I reread a journal entry in which God spoke to me very clearly about trust. God said to me:

"Do you believe that I hear you? Do you believe I want all that is good for you? Do you believe I will answer you? Yes? Then trust me.

"You may think you are walking on a road less traveled, on a path that has not been cleared, and you are. You are because you believe in me. But look up. Just as you take a step, I clear the brambles and bushes away and your path is clear.

"One step at a time, my beloved. Trust me. I see all and know exactly where your path must go in order to draw you closer to me. So follow me and trust."

24

Is the
Single Life
Really a Vocation?

When we think of the word *vocation,* we most often think of a call to the priesthood or sisterhood. Praying for vocations, we ask God to provide the priests and nuns necessary for the future of the Church.

In recent years, however, it seems that this word is being used to indicate a Christlike approach to whatever state in life we live — married, religious, clerical, or single. While people readily refer to marriage, priesthood, and religious life as vocations, I wonder how many people consider the single life to be a "real" vocation. I wonder how many singles consider their way of life to be a vocation.

While the entrance into marriage, priesthood, and religious life is marked by a special ceremony, entrance into the single life is not. A couple sets the date and prepares for the wedding day. A priest plans for his ordination, a Sister or Brother for religious profession. What marks the beginning of the single vocation?

Married couples celebrate their anniversaries, priests and religious their jubilees. What benchmark does the single vocation have? Most important, Christian married couples, priests, Brothers, and Sisters make their commitments before God *and* a community of believers who pledge their prayers and support. When single Christians make a commitment to live their single lives for God, how does the community witness, support, and pray for them in this vocation?

So I ask, is the single life really a vocation?

The single "vocation" is the only vocation someone can receive without choosing it. A person must make a conscious choice to be married, to be ordained, or to join a religious community; but the single state in life is inherited by all at birth. Often, those who remain single find themselves with the single "vocation" out of default, having never consciously chosen it. At what point does the single life based on circumstance become the single vocation based on choice?

The heartbreak for many is that their first choice never came about. An unhappy single wrote, "After fifteen years of novenas, I am still single." For many reasons, some people never had the opportunity to live any way but as a single person. The right mate never came along. Poor health barred entry into a religious community. Caring for an infirm parent left no time for dating. Because of circumstances, many Christian singles are left with one choice: whether or not to commit the single life they live to a single vocation they live for God.

Other single people are unwilling to make a firm commitment to the single state in life. Since single living is more readily accepted today than in the past, many single Christians are delaying decisions to marry or enter religious communities until later in life. Many are also finding themselves struggling to answer the question one single letter writer asked me, "How does one reconcile feelings of wanting to devote one's self totally to God with the hidden longing for a husband and children?" I ask yet another question, "How can one be sure that living the single life is not a choice based on a hidden fear of making a commitment?"

These are difficult questions. I do not know the answers for myself, much less for anyone else. We must each search our own heart and turn to God for the insight that gives us the freedom to answer these questions honestly. We must acknowledge that God's vocational call to us will probably not come like a bolt of lightning as it did for Saint Paul or like the crucifix speaking to Saint Francis of Assisi or even as the gentle tap on the shoulder we might prefer.

Discernment is difficult. It demands much prayer, patience, and courage. Discernment of the single, priestly, or religious vocation is particularly difficult because God's call is not verbalized by another person saying, "Let's get married," as it is for the vocation of marriage. Deciding to respond to a call to a vowed religious vocation or to the single vocation also seems more difficult because the moment of reckoning can be rather elusive. When is the ultimate question asked and when must I answer?

It is sometimes hard to distinguish a call to a vowed religious vocation from a call to the single vocation. One reader phrased it this way in a letter to me: "I felt a calling. At first I thought it was a call to the vowed religious life, but then I realized it was a call to oneness with God through the single life. I am seeking ways to pass this gift of oneness along."

Her letter clarified for me the distinction between the *vowed* religious vocation and the religious living that is essential for all Christians. While God calls some people to the vowed religious life, all Christians are invited to respond to Jesus' call to *a* religious life — to oneness with him — regardless of the vocation they choose. Through Baptism, Eucharist, and Confirmation, Christians make and reaffirm their commitment to God and to the Christian community which in turn pledges to support them in this effort.

It is important to note the adjective *vowed* before religious life. Singles who are trying to discern whether they are being called to a vowed religious vocation or to the single vocation need to take note of this. Professing the vows of poverty, chastity, and obedience and making a commitment to a specific religious community carry with them many obligations. A person committed to God in a single vocation does not have quite these same constraints.

Single people who choose to live their lives for the Lord — within a lifestyle that includes such things as career, home, care for parents, and other worldly obligations — are called to a life of chastity, but they do not have to take the vows of poverty or obedience. On the other hand, they will not have a committed community of vowed religious to support them in this lifestyle. They will have to find support among the general Christian faithful.

More and more opportunities are emerging or gaining renewed exposure which allow singles to remain in the everyday, working world yet become attached to a Christian community above and beyond their parish. These include secular institutes, lay apostolates, Cursillo programs, and covenant charismatic communities. Some of these options include a type of vowed commitment while others do not.

Single Christians do have choices. Through prayer and the assistance of a spiritual director, we can discern God's call in our lives. Through the communion of spirits — God's and our own — we co-create our destinies and vocations. God directs our lives, he does not determine them. We have to do our part.

As singles we must remember that every vocation has elements of joy and sacrifice. No vocation is total bliss. No vocation is without its crosses. Whichever vocation we choose, Jesus' words to his disciples apply to us, his current disciples: "If a man wishes to come after me, he must deny his very self, take up his cross, and follow in my steps. Whoever would preserve his life will lose it, but whoever loses his life for my sake and the gospel's will preserve it" (Mark 8:34-35).

God will give us the strength to carry the crosses of whatever vocation we choose. With God's grace we can let go of our desires for a spouse and children in order to follow his call to be a religious or priest. Guided by the Holy Spirit we can find ways to fulfill our need and desire to be alone with the Lord even if we choose to marry and raise a family. Remaining single and relying on Jesus, we can cope with loneliness and find a Christian community that actively supports the single vocation.

Is the single life really a vocation? My answer is "yes." It becomes a vocation when we freely choose to live our single lives for the Lord, regardless of why we are single.

No one can choose our vocation for us. With Jesus, we must take up our cross and follow him. In the end, it really matters little which vocation we pick, which call we answer, which path we walk. What matters is that we freely choose to follow in his footsteps, in joy and sacrifice, praying as we go:

"Happy they who dwell in your house!
    continually they praise you.
Happy the men whose strength you are!
    their hearts are set upon the pilgrimage. . . .
They go from strength to strength;
    they shall see the God of gods in Zion."
(Psalm 84:5-6,8)

25

When Others Marry

Thoughts churned in my mind as I slowly turned for the seamstress pinning up the hem on my bridesmaid dress. *Could this really be my sixth bridesmaid dress? Am I always to be the bridesmaid, never the bride? Surely I should have been a bride by now. I caught the bouquet the last time I was a bridesmaid. So much for that tradition!* With that, I looked in the mirror.

I have been bridesmaid, lector, and keeper of the guestbook at weddings. I have been the friend of the bride and the sister of the groom and vice versa. I have hosted surprise bridal showers and joined friends for one last singles' night on the town. I have been intimately involved in the planning of several weddings. For others I have traveled hundreds of miles just to be present at the ceremony. I have danced at receptions until my feet hurt and delighted at the reunion of friends and family in the festive spirit that only a wedding can create.

I have shared in the joy, the novelty, the excitement, and the fun of weddings in many different ways and more times than I can begin to count. But after the rice has been thrown and I go home alone one more time, I often hear myself ask, *What about me, Lord?*

Recently, that question resurfaced when I read the wedding invitation of a man I used to date. While we had mutually agreed to end the relationship a couple of years ago, the news of his marriage tugged at my heart. Having known friends who were devastated when past lovers married, I was glad my heart was only pricked with the question, ''What about me, Lord?'' and not stabbed with unrequited love.

Sometimes I feel as though I am standing on the sidelines of a game called *Marriage*. It is hard to be relegated to the sidelines when everyone else seems to be on the field. It is especially hard since I feel I am ready to play. I have seniority over many people that the "Coach" has sent and continues to send onto the field. The question, "What about me, Lord?" becomes a plea, "Come on, Lord, I'm ready to play."

The Lord has responded, "In my time. For now, just keep watching." Sometimes patiently, sometimes not so patiently, I have watched from the sidelines and learned a lot about marriage.

Watching others marry and celebrate anniversaries, I have become more aware of what it takes to play in the *game* of marriage. I have become more aware, and consequently more determined, to learn the skills necessary to stay in the game, whenever I am given the chance to play.

Marriage takes practice. It is not mastered overnight. It requires teamwork, cooperation, and compromise. It can be full of excitement and tension or boring and slow-moving. It demands commitment, perseverance, and patience.

I have seen all this from the sidelines, and more. I have seen how the transition from single life to married life can be difficult and uncomfortable. I realize that the longer I am single, the longer this transition will likely take if I marry.

I have observed a newly married friend write "we" instead of "I" in her letters, and I have sensed the change in our relationship. The naïveté of youth that said things don't have to change has been replaced by the acceptance of the reality that friendships do and must change when a friend gets married.

My years on the sidelines have deepened my desire to be married. I yearn to be united with another person and thereby to feel complete. Thanks to prayer, this feeling has matured. As I have grown closer to Jesus, he has revealed to me that I may have been seeking something in marriage that only God can give.

The desire to be fulfilled through the union with a spouse is definitely part of the motivation for marrying, but I can never be totally united or satisfied by another human being. The hunger for wholeness within the depths of my soul can only be satisfied by God, and only in fleeting moments until the day I am eternally united with him.

Jesus has often reminded me of this truth as he has directed me to read and reread his prayer for us, recorded in John's Gospel:

"that all may be one
as you, Father, are in me, and I in you;
I pray that they may be [one] in us."
(John 17:21)

By meditating on these words, my expectations of marriage and of a spouse have been put into perspective — Jesus' perspective.

For me, Jesus' perspective in marriage also means that the person I marry must believe in Jesus. My criteria for "Mr. Right" used to be quite long and specific. Now I merely pray for a husband who will be my best friend and want me to be his and that we will share each other's personal relationship with Jesus in a deep and intimate way. As for the other qualifications, I leave them up to Jesus.

From the sidelines I have watched some people marry and stay in the game and others marry and then lose through divorce. I am even more convinced that if I hope to stay in the game of marriage, my future husband and I must not only believe in Jesus but also acknowledge that he is our Coach. We must rely on Jesus for the strategy, the encouragement, the correction, and the support to persevere and win in the marriage game.

Marriage is demanding because the world around us and within us is full of struggles and temptations. The vow of love in sickness and in health, in good times and in bad is awesome. I can't imagine myself keeping this vow without relying on Jesus to fill in where my human nature and the human nature of others fall short. Marriage takes more than two; it takes three. I believe Jesus must be more than a team player; he must be the Coach.

By watching from the sidelines, I have grown to appreciate God's timing. Still, my patience periodically wears thin. "Come on, Lord, it's my turn. I want to play."

And Jesus says, "Your heavenly Father knows all that you need. Seek first his kingship over you, his way of holiness, and all these things will be given you besides" (Matthew 6:32-33).

Those who, like me, are watching, waiting, and wondering if they will ever marry can take comfort in those words from

Matthew's Gospel. Our Father knows what we want. He knows our hearts better than we know ourselves. He hears our pleas, and he promises to answer. He asks us to show our love and our faith in him by seeking his reign in our hearts. Only through Jesus can we hope to meet and marry someone who knows and loves him too. This will only happen through Jesus, so we must seek him and his kingship in our lives.

If it is God's will that I marry, and if I sincerely seek to do his will, then I know I will marry in God's good time. If it is not God's will, then he must have something better in store for me, because Jesus assures me, ''Your Father knows all that you need.''

Let's be hopeful as we watch from the sidelines. Be joyful when others marry. Remember it is never too late to marry. Two years ago a friend in her fifties married for the first time. The other day I met a husband and wife who were both in their eighties. They were talking about celebrating their twenty-fourth wedding anniversary. These people watched from the sidelines for many years before entering the game.

If it is the Father's will for us, and if we sincerely seek his kingship, we can be assured that someday, in his perfect timing, the Coach will send us on the field. In the meantime, let's live the single life peacefully and happily united to Jesus, our model for single living.

26

What About Children?

It often hits me out of the blue. I can be walking through a museum, and instead of looking at the exhibits I catch myself watching children toddle along next to their parents. Or I find myself in church, gazing into the eyes of a child in the pew in front of me and giving a rote response to the priest at the altar.

Holding a niece or nephew, wandering through the infants' clothing section of a department store, receiving Christmas cards from friends with pictures showing not one, but two, three, and four children, all have a way of bringing my desire for children vividly to my attention.

Children have always been an important part of my life. I was an avid baby-sitter as a teenager and a governess one summer during my college years. I have enjoyed cuddling infants, chasing after toddlers, picnicking with grade schoolers, and teaching swimming and ice skating to children of all ages. Despite the reputation teenagers have, I have enjoyed watching their baseball and soccer games, helping shop for their prom dresses, and even listening to their music, albeit in small doses.

My single lifestyle has separated me from day-to-day exposure to children. A job in an office and a social life with my single peers have kept me running in circles that don't naturally intersect with kids. In the early stages of my single life I didn't really notice this. As I have grown older, however, I have noticed the lack of children in my life. I have also become increasingly aware of my desire to be around children and, specifically, children of my own.

The question arises naturally, "What about children?"

What about children when you are single and the biological clock is ticking louder each year? What about children if the biological alarm has already sounded and the desire is still there? What about children when you have made a commitment to a celibate vocation but love to be with kids?

A growing number of single women have answered the question by adopting a child. In recent years there has been a dramatic increase in the number of single women adopting children. Statistics indicate that the desire for children and the choice to adopt is more prevalent among single women than single men, but many single men are also struggling with the question, "What about children?"

While the desire for children is burning within me, I do not consider adoption to be a solution for quenching it. I have observed too many friends who are emotionally and financially struggling with their role as single mothers for me to choose this lifestyle. For this reason I have rejected an option that appears to be an answer for many in today's society. Now what?

I turn to Jesus in search of my answer. I turn to him who was also a single person with an obvious love for children. Jesus is recorded in the Gospels of Matthew, Mark, and Luke as gathering the children around him, even as the disciples tried to shoo them away. "Let the children come to me. Do not hinder them. The kingdom of God belongs to such as these. And he laid his hands on their heads before he left that place" (Matthew 19:14-15).

Jesus liked to be around children. He talked to them, embraced them, blessed them, healed them, and promised his kingdom to them. They were a special part of his life, despite the fact that he had no children of his own. He must have longed to be a father, even as I long to be a mother.

Feeling that Jesus truly empathizes with my human desire for children, I beg him for his divine answer to my question, "What about children?" I believe he will help me satisfy spiritually what is not being fulfilled physically.

Jesus first reminds me of how much the Father loves me and all humankind. His love is so great that he sent his only Son to live and die among us.

"Yes, God so loved the world
that he gave his only Son,
that whoever believes in him may not die

but may have eternal life.''
(John 3:16)

God expressed his love in flesh and instilled in humans this same instinct and desire to see their love become flesh in their sons and daughters. My desire for children springs from the maternal instinct God the Father created in me and from an overflowing love that, like his own, seeks expression in the flesh.

This desire for children, while initially a painful hunger, has become a means by which Jesus has drawn me closer to himself and to his Father. I am more in touch with the human Jesus and the feelings and desires I share with him. Through Jesus I now feel a special oneness with the Father, whose love for me is manifest in his Son. This love now overflows in me, his daughter, and reaches out to others.

How do I, as a single Christian, express my love and the Father's love within me in the flesh?

Quite simply, I love other people's children. I present myself to my loving Father as an instrument of his love in the lives of others, and especially others' children.

First, I make the most out of being an aunt and godmother. Though I am miles away, I show my interest in the lives of my nieces and my nephew by calling, by writing, by visiting. I cherish the stories their parents tell me, the photographs they send me, and the times we are together. What a delightful surprise it is for this single aunt to pick up the phone and hear a two-year-old's squeaky voice breathlessly say, ''Hi, Aunt Martha.''

Closer to home, I baby-sit for the children of my single-parent and married friends when they need a weekend away. I am often able to love their children in a way that only an outsider to the household can love them. I romp with the little ones, make ice cream with the mid-size group, and let the older ones drive my car. Sometimes, just being there, as they run in and out of the house on their way to somewhere else, says that I care. Too many times, their single or working parents can't do that.

Across the continents, I also express my love for children. Through prayer and fasting, I remember the hungry, homeless, abandoned, and abused children of the world. Through letters and charitable contributions I also love them. I have ''adopted'' a young girl who is a refugee from Tibet living in India. Her letters thanking me for the food on her family's table, her Bible, and her new clothes, tell me God is truly using me as his instrument of love. I feel his love and her love, as I read the handwritten sign-off on her letters, "Your loving child."

I also reach out in love to unborn children and their mothers who might have preferred the situation to be different. Working for an organization called Hope of Northern Virginia, I have answered the crisis calls of women with problem pregnancies. I have counseled a teenager through the agonizing decision of whether to keep her baby or to give it up for adoption. I send money to this organization and others attempting to help troubled women answer the question, "What about children?" for themselves. I pray for these women, that they may answer it with a respect for their children — the love and life of God they carry in a special way within them.

What about children? Whether or not I ever have any of my own, Jesus gives me many opportunities to be with children, to love them, and to be loved by them. What's more, he reminds me, "Whoever welcomes a child such as this for my sake welcomes me. And whoever welcomes me, welcomes not me, but him who sent me" (Mark 9:37).

27

Free to
Love Many

She had been my high school religion teacher, but at the age of twenty-six I was still her student. We were discussing vocations, and she mentioned something that I had not realized before and have not forgotten since. "Because we are not committed to love one, we are free to love many."

Free to love many. She and I were both free to love many because she, as a nun, and I, as a single, were not committed to loving a spouse and children.

But what does "free to love many" really mean? Why do the single, the vowed religious, and the priestly vocations have this freedom, whereas the married vocation does not? As Christians, are we not all called to love others, and many others, regardless of vocation?

Saint Paul provides insight into these questions in his First Letter to the Corinthians: "I should like you to be free of all worries. The unmarried man is busy with the Lord's affairs, concerned with pleasing the Lord; but the married man is busy with this world's demands and occupied with pleasing his wife. This means he is divided. The virgin — indeed, any unmarried woman — is concerned with things of the Lord, in pursuit of holiness in body and spirit. The married woman, on the other hand, has the cares of this world to absorb her and is concerned with pleasing her husband" (1 Corinthians 7:32-34).

It is not that married Christians are less dedicated to loving and serving the Lord than single or vowed religious Christians. Rather, married people must expend the major portion of their efforts and their love to care for their spouse and those who are dependent upon them.

As a single person with no dependents, I am bound to no one. I have neither the responsibilities nor the expectations for another. No spouse or children are counting on me to put food on the table, clothes on their backs, a roof over their heads, or a hug around their shoulders. As a single Christian who is neither a single parent nor a single person caring for aging parents, I am free to love God with an undivided heart and to respond to God's love by loving others in ways married Christians or singles with dependents are not free to do.

Comparing my life to the lives of my married siblings has deepened my appreciation of this freedom to love many. It is not a comparison to determine which is the best. Rather, it is a look at how our lives and our responses to God are different.

My two older sisters are both wives and mothers. They are both blessed with caring husbands and beautiful, healthy children. One is a physical therapist, the other a first grade teacher, though presently they have both chosen to be full-time mothers.

Recently, they both experienced significant changes in their lifestyles. Their husbands changed jobs. One sister's spouse is now working late-night hours. The other sister's husband travels constantly. During the tension-filled transitions they are presently undergoing, they have both assumed additional responsibilities in their homes and marriages. They are making adjustments cheerfully and energetically, at least most of the time, because of the vow they took on their wedding day to love and honor their husbands. Likewise, their husbands are striving to fulfill their vows to their wives, especially in their current roles as primary breadwinners, loving husbands, and devoted fathers.

I also have two married brothers. One is a captain in the US Army, the other just finished law school and is the father of a daughter. Their decisions and lifestyles also have reflected their marriage vows. The captain was faced with deciding whether he would make a career in the army or resign and take a job in the private sector. Had he been single, I don't think the decision would have been as difficult to make. He and his wife have had to seriously consider the effects that transfers would have on her career and how long periods of separation would affect their marriage and their future family.

The lawyer had dreams of applying his expertise as a prosecuting attorney. He was faced with the decision of waiting for an opening in a department in our hometown or taking a position that was offered by a private firm fifty miles away. Had he been single, he might even have explored other options. Since he and his family had lived on a shoestring during the three years he attended law school, he accepted the offer that would put food on the table over the dream that would not.

I respect my sisters and brothers for the decisions they have made for themselves and their families. I admire how they are loving God, their spouses, children, friends, neighbors, and community through their married vocations. At the same time, I see the truth in what Saint Paul says, ''The married man is busy with this world's demands and occupied with pleasing his wife. . . . The married woman has the cares of this world to absorb her and is concerned with pleasing her husband.''

Because I have neither a spouse nor children depending on me, I am free to do many things my siblings cannot do. I still have many cares, but they are principally for my well-being. When I hear God's call to move to a new city, to take a new job, or to write a book, I have the freedom to decide and to act as I will, without concern for the responsibilities for or expectations of others.

For example, I was up at 4:30 A.M. every day in order to write this book and still hold a full-time job. My sister is up in the wee hours of the morning and is busy throughout the day caring for her baby. Selflessly, my sister is the loving one. It is my hope and prayer that through this book I am sharing God's love with many.

I am free to spend entire weekends baby-sitting a friend's family, with no concern for what I may have left undone in my own home. For a year, my other married sister has juggled the responsibilities of her own home and family with those of a neighbor who became seriously ill and needed someone to help care for her three children.

I bought a house five miles from work. This short commute means my free time can be devoted to writing or volunteer work. My brother spends two hours a day commuting to his office so that his family may continue to live in familiar surroundings as they await the birth of their second child.

I can spend hours volunteering, listening to a friend who needs to talk, writing letters, or praying for our troubled world. My sisters and brothers, who might try to do similar things, are often interrupted by a cry, by a child who wants to play, by a telephone call saying "I'll be late," by a timer on the stove, or by a buzzer on the dryer. Their efforts may be further complicated by the need to find reliable baby-sitters and money to pay them.

In our own ways, we all are loving God and others. It is obvious to me, however, that singles do have the freedom of time, energy, money, and emotions to love many because they are not committed to loving and caring for a few.

Because single Christians are so free to love many, we must be on our guard against allowing this freedom to disproportionately rule our lives. It is important that we prayerfully discern how, when, and where God is calling us to love many lest our efforts to love become compulsive and fragmented.

I make this point because I have seen several single Christians become obsessed with giving and doing for others to the detriment of their own health, jobs, and overall well-being. I have seen myself dash from one "good work" to another until I became drained and ineffective. I have had the best of intentions, but whose intentions were they — mine or God's?

When I stopped to ask this question, the image of a wild horse came to my mind. A wild horse may be strong, of good stock, and beautiful to watch as it runs freely. An equally strong horse, tamed and tethered to a wagon or a plow, accomplishes a given task with the same energy the wild horse expends dashing where it will.

I realized I had been like the wild horse, dashing about, loving others, and serving the needs of many people. I did this thinking I was following God's will. When I finally stopped to ask him if I was, and to allow him to tame me and direct me, I found myself tethered to a modern-day plow — the word processor — with the task of writing this particular book and loving many through this work.

I call attention to another characteristic of the single Christian's freedom to love many — expectation. Since marriage is a commitment between two people, each person pledges his or her love to the other. With the marriage vow, therefore, comes the expectation that each person will be loved.

I often hear married couples discuss their theories about what should be the percentage of giving and receiving in the relationship

. . . fifty/fifty, ninety/ten, one hundred/one hundred. Ideally, it would be nice if each partner gave one hundred percent to the other. Regardless of percentage, however, there will always be an element of expectation in the marriage relationship.

Since I have not vowed to love another in the bond of marriage, and since no one has made the vow to love me, I cannot expect someone to love me exclusively. In many respects, Jesus has made it easier for Christian singles to grow in the ability to love as he loves — unconditionally and freely — because there is no one person we can justifiably expect to love us in return.

Obviously, I still need to be loved. I have, in fact, often had unfair expectations and hopes that a friend or family member would love me as I needed to be loved. I have been disappointed. Through this disappointment I learned that I cannot ignore my needs or pretend I have no expectations. I must, instead, give them to Jesus and ask him for the love I need. I must also come to a deeper realization that he is always giving me this love, even before I ask for it. In the security of his love, I have been given the power and freedom to strive to love many unconditionally.

As Christian singles, we are indeed free to love many. We must constantly turn to Jesus for his guidance and love so that we may love those he wants and needs us to love in the unconditional way he calls us to love.

Saint Francis captured the essence of unconditional love in his prayer for peace. It is appropriate for all vocations, and especially for single Christians as we capitalize on our freedom to love many.

Lord, make me an instrument of your peace.
Where there is hatred, let me sow love;
Where there is injury, pardon;
Where there is doubt, faith;
Where there is despair, hope;
Where there is darkness, light;
And where there is sadness, joy.
O Divine Master, grant that I may not so much seek to be consoled
    as to console; to be understood as to understand; to be loved as
    to love. For it is in giving that we receive, it is in pardoning that
    we are pardoned, and it is in dying that we are born to eternal
    life."

28

Celebrating
the Single Life

Who said the single life has no special days to celebrate like weddings and ordinations, anniversaries and jubilees? Who said? I have said this, and so have other singles.

Single people have shared with me, in person and through letters, that they feel years come and go without much notice. While they may enjoy the single life, they still feel a void, a sorrow because there are no days of celebration for the single life.

Much of this is due to the fact that society calls attention to all sorts of days that exclude singles except as gift givers: weddings, anniversaries, Mother's Day, and Father's Day. As singles, we remember these days with joy, love, and celebration for and with others. In return, what days do others mark as special for us?

Singles have birthdays to celebrate, but for many singles a birthday is a painful day rather than one of celebration. Like their married and religious peers, many singles find growing old difficult, especially when no one remembers their birthdays.

Even the Church has special days that tend to exclude singles. Sunday liturgies celebrating marriage and the family are a beautiful part of parish community life that tends to leave singles out, unless someone is a single parent. Baptism, First Communion, Confirmation, Matrimony, and Ordination are days of celebration for the recipients of these sacraments and their families. Even religious communities gather together to celebrate the feast days of their patron saints, foundresses, or founders. Are there any religious or sacramental celebrations that note the uniqueness of the single life and vocation?

There are no sacraments unique to the single vocation, but God opened my eyes to the opportunities he gives me to celebrate my singleness with him and with others.

Several years ago, I participated in a Cursillo "retreat" weekend. It was probably one of the most freeing religious experiences I have had as an adult. Jesus drew me closer to him and to others that weekend. I experienced his love in a deeper way and felt this reflected in a community of believers that loved me unconditionally. I was introduced to a new world of prayer and community life. It was such a benchmark in my life, and in my spiritual journey, that I shall always remember the dates: March 4, 5, and 6.

These dates took on additional significance as I prepared to write this book. I became aware of my need to seek God's Spirit of wisdom and inspiration in a profound way. I decided to take a day off from work and spend twenty-four hours in prayer and fasting at the Madonna House not far from my home. I set a date, but then was forced to change it due to developments on the job. Finally, I identified another break in my schedule and took the day off.

I set everything aside for a day, and entered a room with only the bare essentials: a bed, a desk, a cross, a picture of the Blessed Mother, my Bible, and my journal. It was a restful and revealing "desert experience" with Jesus, which propelled me into the full-fledged writing of this book with a Holy Spirit-infused confidence.

Toward the end of this day of prayer, I realized it was March 5. My heart was filled with the joy of the present experience and overflowed upon realizing Jesus and I had just celebrated the anniversary of a memorable moment in *our* past.

Then I realized that singles do have special events to remember and anniversaries to mark. We just need to take the time to look at our lives through Jesus' eyes. If we prayerfully reflect upon the special moments we have shared with Christ, we may discover days to celebrate. If we discover special moments in our past, we can be sure Jesus has more to come in our future if we continue to seek him.

We can remember not only days but also places. How many times have you heard people recall memories of something shared in a particular place? Thanks to my relationship with Jesus, I now go places where my first thought is, "Jesus, remember when we wrote in the sand (or gazed at the sunset or inhaled the mountain air)?'' Such memories are tied to places close to home and far away.

Whenever I meander through the Iwo Jima Park near my home, I am reminded of the days I sat with Jesus gazing at the view of the magnificent monuments in our nation's capital. One time he inspired me with the theme for a speech I was writing. Another time we discussed whether it was time to move, and I pleaded to stay. If and when I again feel the urge to move, I will seek out this place to prayerfully discern my decision.

A few hours from home there is a cabin where I once spent three days in solitary retreat. I never step into that cabin or walk along the nearby beach without remembering the days I spent in intimate communion with my God.

Much farther from home is a place that comes to my mind every Good Friday. The place is called *Ecce Homo* and is located under a convent on the Via Dolorosa in Jerusalem. It is thought to be the site where Jesus was crowned with thorns and mocked by the soldiers. Hearing the reading of the Gospels during Holy Week, I recall my poignant moments in prayer at this place, where the stark reality of Jesus' Passion touched me in a way I shall never forget.

Jesus has given me many special moments to remember and celebrate with him, but he has also given me moments to celebrate with others. Holding my nephew and answering the questions reserved for the godparent, I again experienced the wonder and meaning of Baptism. I was not being baptized, but God's graces filled me even as they were pouring out on my godson. Thankfully, these graces continue to flow as my relationship with my nephew grows in fun and in faith despite the 500 miles that separate us.

This bond with my godson has given Mother's Day new significance. I may not be a mother, but through my sister and my sister's son I have tasted the joy of motherhood. While I may not be remembered on Mother's Day, I remember my mother, my sisters, and many other friends and family with deeper feelings for my having experienced motherhood as a godmother.

I have also been privileged to be the sponsor for an adult friend when he was confirmed and welcomed as a member of the Catholic Church. I was filled with joy when he and his wife asked me to be his sponsor. His Confirmation was a memorable event for me. Again I felt the flow of the Holy Spirit, as I witnessed another person experience the grace of a sacrament.

Whether we serve as godparents, sponsors, witnesses at a wedding, or readers at an ordination, we singles are given opportunities to intimately experience God's love in the sacraments even though another person actually celebrates the sacrament.

In big ways and little ways, on special days and in special places, Jesus invites us to share and celebrate our single lives with him and with others. By responding to his invitation we hope to experience his Last Supper wish for us, "That my joy may be yours and your joy may be complete" (John 15:11).

29

Marching to a Different Beat

Do you ever feel out of step with the world? Do you ever feel you are marching to the beat of a different drummer? It seems the more I have sought Jesus in every facet of my life, the more I have had to struggle with marching to a different beat.

I struggle because I *long to belong*. I long to be like those around me and to feel connected to them. I am not unique in this longing. Other people long to belong too. If they didn't, why would family unity be so highly valued? Why would people gather in neighborhoods and churches? What about bridge clubs and service clubs? Look at our emphasis on patriotism in America, and our participation in the United Nations.

The current increase in the number of cults tells me that our society's ever-expanding list of groups still does not fill the bill for many people. Many people are willing to forfeit their freedom and individuality in the hope of filling the basic human need I call *longing to belong*.

While I long to belong, I have also chosen to follow Jesus. Because of my choice, I am marching to a different beat. I feel as though I don't completely belong to the world around me. As I stand up for what I believe and strive to follow Jesus by living and sharing his Word, I often feel misunderstood and rejected. Sometimes I feel like an outcast, an oddity.

These feelings are not unique to me either. The Scriptures are filled with stories of prophets and kings who listened to Yahweh and obeyed his call, only to find themselves ostracized and persecuted. Elijah cried out, "I have been most zealous for the LORD, the God of hosts. But the Israelites have forsaken your covenant, torn down your altars, and put your prophets to the sword. I alone am left, and they seek to take my life'' (1 Kings 19:14).

In anguish, the psalmist prayed:

"Since for your sake I bear insult
    and shame covers my face.
I have become an outcast to my brothers,
    a stranger to my mother's sons.
They who sit at the gate gossip about me,
    and drunkards make me the butt of their songs."
(Psalm 69:8-9,13)

Almost to the point of despair, Jeremiah pleaded:

"All the day I am an object of laughter;
    everyone mocks me.
The word of the LORD has brought me
    derision and reproach."
(Jeremiah 20:7,8)

The Word of the Lord has often brought me derision and reproach, which in turn has heightened my sense of not belonging to the world around me. At work I have been chided by colleagues for going to daily Mass, despite my effort to do so without notice. Promotion opportunities in one office ended when I stood firm on my Christian principles when they were challenged. On the social scene, I have been ridiculed, rejected, and physically threatened when I refused to give in to the sexual pressure exerted by men I have dated. People I thought were my friends have ended friendships because they became uncomfortable with the intensity with which I live my Christian faith. Like Jeremiah, I have been tempted to say:

"I will not mention him,
    I will speak in his name no more."
(Jeremiah 20:9)

But Jesus is quick to remind me that persecution and rejection are part of being his disciple.

"If you find that the world hates you,
know it has hated me before you.
If you belonged to the world,
it would love you as its own;
the reason it hates you
is that you do not belong to the world.
But I chose you out of the world."
(John 15:18-19)

Jesus chose us out of the world to belong to him and his Father. He chose us to be his witnesses, to carry forth his mission, and bring about his kingdom on earth. Because we said "yes" to his call and because we believe in his name, we do not really belong to the world. We can expect to be misunderstood and persecuted as Jesus was because "No slave is greater than his master" (John 15:20).

As followers of Jesus we do not belong to the world, but in the power of his name we belong to each other. By joining together in the Church — Christ's Body on earth — we have the opportunity to give and receive sustenance, strength, courage, and a sense of belonging. This empowers us to give witness to Jesus in word and deed, despite the world's rejection.

We must follow Jesus' example and surround ourselves with people who share our faith and mission. Even as Jesus gathered together with his apostles, we too must gather together with his present-day disciples.

As we grow in our relationship with Jesus and in our awareness of his love for us, we will also grow in our love for one another. This love will not only sustain us and satisfy our longing to belong but also strengthen our witness in the world.

"No one has ever seen God.
Yet if we love one another
God dwells in us,
and his love is brought to perfection in us."
(1 John 4:12)

If a large group of people stand up and proclaim that they belong to each other in love, the world will have to take notice. As Christians, our gift, our witness to the world is that we belong to one another through Jesus. Belonging to Jesus and to each other we form the Church and offer this sense of belonging to the world. "Through him the whole body grows, and with the proper functioning of the members joined firmly together by each supporting ligament, builds itself up in love" (Ephesians 4:16).

It is for this reason, if no other, that single Christians must remain committed to the Church, even though the Church often forgets about them. We must participate in *our* Church and raise the consciousness of our fellow Christians because we are one with them through Christ. If we want the world to see how Christians love one another, then, as single Christians, we must join others and make the Church into the loving community, the loving witness intended by Jesus. We also need the support of the Christian community to sustain us and give us a sense of belonging, as we march to the beat that the world rejects.

As we march to Jesus' beat, the world will continue to persecute us as individuals and as a Church because it persecuted Jesus. Even as we continue to profess our faith in word and deed, let us join together and give witness in prayer, in worship, in support, in strength, and in love. Let us seek Jesus and his community of followers when we feel misunderstood and rejected by the world which does not know him. Then, let us return to the world and convert it to Christ.

What is most important, let us remember Jesus' promise, "Blest shall you be when men hate you, when they ostracize you and insult you and proscribe your name as evil because of the Son of Man. On the day they do so, rejoice and exult, for your reward shall be great in heaven" (Luke 6:22-23).

It is in heaven, united with God the Father, Son, and Holy Spirit, and all God's people, that the beat will stop and our longing to belong will be finally and completely satisfied.

30

Keeping My Eyes
on Jesus

The lake was calm and the breeze balmy as the boat pulled away from the dock. The surrounding countryside was dry and barren, offering little dimension or contrast in this photographer's eye, so I put my camera away. The sun burned warmth into my face, and the shimmery water made me squint and close my eyes. It was in a spirit of reflection that I journeyed across the Sea of Galilee.

Events of Jesus' life which took place near the Sea of Galilee have always struck a chord in me — especially two incidents that involved Peter. On that quiet boat ride between Tiberias and Capernaum, they once again came to mind.

I identify with the call of Peter in Luke's Gospel where Jesus gets into Peter's boat and instructs him to push out from shore and drop his nets. After some objection, Peter does as Jesus directs and proceeds to catch so many fish that he is frightened by the miraculous power of the man seated in his boat. Peter pleads, "Leave me, Lord. I am a sinful man." Jesus assures him, "Do not be afraid. From now on you will be catching men" (Luke 5:8,10).

While sitting in a boat on the Sea of Galilee, I reflected on Peter's call and realized this scene had occurred in my life. Growing up in a secure, religious family environment and attending Catholic school, I have always taken it for granted that Jesus was in my boat. It was not until I entered the business world and began to write for publication and speak before large groups of people that I first heard Jesus instruct me to drop my nets.

Initially, I objected. I was not trained in journalism or literature, and I lacked confidence. I did not particularly enjoy writing. I found it a difficult and lonely task. When I finally consented, Jesus filled my portfolio to overflowing with published columns, speeches, and a small book.

My nets were so overflowing that I heard Jesus ask, "Martha, will you write for me?" Like Peter, I fell to my knees, "Go away from me, Lord. I am a sinful woman." Jesus assured me, "Have no fear. I will give you the words"; but I was still too frightened to say "yes."

It took several years of prayer and the affirmation of many people before I found the courage to say "yes." I was slow to trust that Jesus would guide me in my writing. When I finally submitted several articles to a religious magazine, I received the positive, professional reinforcement that Jesus knew I needed.

The *Liguorian* magazine bought article after article that I submitted. I then met with the editors to discuss a theme for a regular singles' feature in the magazine. In time, I began receiving letters from single and married readers, sharing their lives and their hearts with me. My nets were again overflowing.

I began to play with the idea of writing a book for Christian singles, and I wondered if Jesus was calling me again. Turning to the passage of Peter walking on the water, I meditated on Peter's words to Jesus, "Lord, if it is really you, tell me to come to you across the water" (Matthew 14:28).

For me to write a book would be a miracle on a par with Peter's walking on water. I decided to challenge Jesus, "Lord, if it is really you, tell me to write a book for single Christians."

During that quiet ride on the Sea of Galilee Jesus spoke to me. The sea was not stormy and I could not see the Lord across the water, yet in the depths of my soul I heard him say, as he had said to Peter, "Come."

I returned from my Holy Land pilgrimage feeling invited and inspired to write this book. The sea did not always remain calm. It has been a rough walk across the water. More than once I have been overcome by storms around me and within me.

I have had to juggle a full-time job, a marathon travel schedule, dating, and the entertainment of out-of-town guests with a writing schedule that required a pre-dawn alarm every morning and seclusion on many sunny weekends when I would have preferred to be "playing" outside.

I have been plagued by sickness, fatigue, stress, eye strain, a cracked rib, sore hands, and heartache. I have felt frightened and vulnerable in sharing the intimate details of my life and my relationship with Jesus. At times my mind became so jumbled I could not think clearly. I became discouraged, overwhelmed, and anxious.

Near the end, I was tempted to despair, feeling isolated from and forgotten by the very people I was counting on for support. No one seemed to understand what it meant to write a book or why I felt so compelled to follow such a grueling schedule. The storms of self-pity swirled in my soul, and I began to sink. Once again like Peter, I cried out, "Lord, save me."

With gentleness and mercy Jesus stretched out his hand and lifted me. As he did, I realized why I had been sinking. I had lost sight of him. I had let the storms distract me. I had forgotten that it was Jesus' power, not my own, enabling me to walk across the water.

The tears came forth, as I begged for his forgiveness, understanding, and the strength to begin again. He directed me to people who listened to me and loved me, even as they challenged me to continue. He rebuked me as he did Peter, "How little faith you have!" and filled my heart with repentance. He reminded me of people with much deeper suffering than my own and called me to offer mine as intercession for them. He lifted me up, restored my faith, helped me continue my walk across the water, and gave me the concluding message of this book.

The message is captured in the First Letter to Timothy, "This explains why we work and struggle as we do; our hopes are fixed on the living God who is the savior of all men, but especially of those who believe" (1 Timothy 4:10).

We believe that Jesus is our Lord and Savior. Because we believe, we have chosen to march to a different beat, *to enter through the narrow gate*. As we do, we must not forget how Jesus describes our choice, "How narrow is the gate that leads to life, how rough the road, and how few there are who find it!" (Matthew 7:13,14)

The road home to our heavenly Father is difficult. It is painful to pick up our cross and follow Jesus. There are times when the storms of suffering consume us, and other times when the bright sunshine of joy blinds us. Sometimes the journey seems more challenging because we are single.

As single Christians, we must endure the storms and bask in the sunshine of our lifestyle *in Jesus' name*. We must keep our eyes on Jesus as we walk through the storms of loneliness, selfishness, isolation, endless "to do" lists, the longing to belong, the hunger for physical affection and emotional intimacy, and the lack of a spouse and children.

We must keep our eyes on Jesus so that, as we delight in our freedom and independence, in our careers and our good fortune, in our families and friends, in our homes and our travels, we will not lose sight of him. We must keep our eyes on Jesus through prayer and worship, through the Scriptures and the sacraments and Christian community and service to one another.

We must keep our eyes on Jesus. Through faith in Jesus we will successfully sail across the waters of our single lives, whether these waters are choppy or calm. Sometimes Jesus will even call us to step out of the boat and walk across the water. Then more than ever we must keep our eyes on him. Only through his power can we hope to accomplish what he calls each of us to do for him, his Father, and his people.

If there were just one message God wanted to communicate to me and to others through this book, it would be, "Keep your eyes on Jesus." Whatever we do, wherever we are, in the midst of all circumstances, we must keep our eyes on Jesus.

By keeping my eyes on Jesus and by constantly refocusing my vision when I lost sight of him, I risked opening my heart and sharing my search for a deeper awareness of Jesus within myself, in others, and in the world. For the glory of our Father and the enrichment of his people, Jesus gave me the discipline, the strength, and the faith to walk across the water and write this book.

May all of us continue to search. May we all come to know the power of Jesus within us. May we grow in our individual relationships with him so that when he says "Come," we will follow.

Keeping our eyes on Jesus as we search, let us pray for each other in Saint Paul's words to the Ephesians: "May the God of our Lord Jesus Christ, the Father of glory, grant you a spirit of wisdom and insight to know him clearly. May he enlighten your innermost vision that you may know the great hope to which he has called you, the wealth of his glorious heritage to be distributed among the members of the church, and the immeasurable scope of his power in us who believe" (Ephesians 1:17-19).

MORE HELP FOR THE SINGLE CHRISTIAN . . .

UNLOCKING THE DOORS OF YOUR HEART
A New Look at Love
by Russell M. Abata, C.SS.R., S.T.D.

This book presents a full picture of love, clarifying the issues in the ongoing war between the ideas of love and sex. By openly discussing appetites, senses, feelings, and mind and will, it helps the reader see that living is for loving and loving is for living. **$4.25**

CHRISTIAN LIVING
Ten Basic Virtues
by Ralph Ranieri

The author devotes a chapter to each of the ten basic virtues and invites the reader to rediscover the meaning and need for them in today's Christian life. **$1.50**

HOW TO PRAY ALWAYS
(Without Always Praying)
by Silvio E. Fittipaldi

The author, a theologian and spiritual guide, explains that prayer is rooted in basic life experience. Borrowing expertly from Sacred Scripture and from other religious traditions, he focuses on experiences that make us more human and more prayerful. Saint Paul urged us to "pray always." This book will show you how. **$2.95**

INNER CALM
A Christian Answer to Modern Stress
by Dr. Paul DeBlassie, III

This book helps people to heal themselves from the ravages of modern-day stress. The author focuses on its causes and leads readers, step by step, on to deep spiritual experience by use of the time-honored Jesus Prayer. **$3.95**

ONLY YOU CAN MAKE YOU HAPPY
by John C. Tormey

On these pages you will find a collection of 90 prayerful and uplifting thoughts to help you direct your mind toward happiness. **$1.95**